**Created by: Ace Glenn & Blake Nubar**
**Illustrations by: Rachel Whitt**



PO Box 2128
Orlando, FL 32802

www.blakenubar.com

Printed in PRC

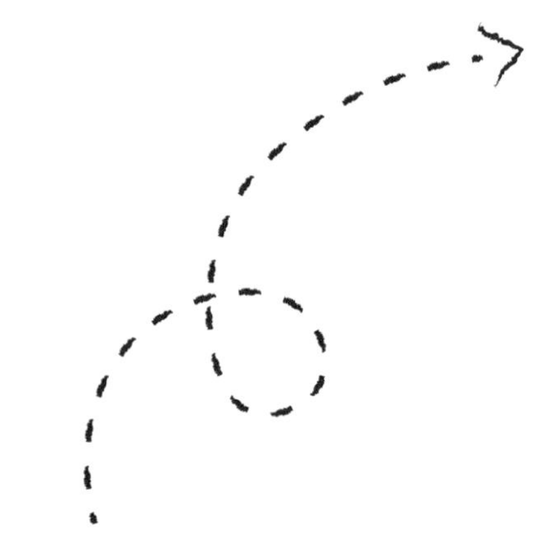

# Let's get started!

## SPECIAL MESSAGE FROM BLAKE!

Congratulations on taking action!

# In your hands right now is the most epic book in the WORLD on starting (or growing) any business with social media...

### WHAT YOU'LL DISCOVER:

- How to instantly launch or grow any business online
- The hidden opportunity on social media
- How to create an irresistible "lead magnet"
- 5 emails that generate revenue on auto-pilot
- Get unlimited FREE leads & sales!

"I have never, in my 2 year entrepreneurial journey, bought a course with **so much value packed into it.**"

- DEVON W.

"This training is the **best thing I've done for my business... maybe ever!** Just follow the steps folks, it's a winner."

- ERIC C.

"**What this training did for me is SO powerful!** I wake up everyday excited about where my business is going to go."

- LISA T.

### SPECIAL VIDEO FROM BLAKE!

Let me show you how this interactive book works and how to get the most out of it!

# Welcome!

Congratulations on getting your hands on this book! If you're reading this, chances are you're an entrepreneur searching for ways to start or grow a business online using social media...

**If that's the case, you're in luck!**

**This book was created to show you a BRAND NEW way to utilize social media to start (or grow) a business online.**

The best part is - this strategy is "set it and forget it." You can set it up once and reap the benefits forever. It's a no-brainer!

And don't worry! It's all 100% beginner proof! Anyone can do this - even if the words "viral" or "landing page" scare the heck out of you.

Ready to get started?

# Who is this book for?

This book was created for anyone who wants to start (or grow) any type of business online!

**DEPENDING ON YOUR SPECIFIC GOALS, YOU PROBABLY FALL INTO 1 OF 2 CATEGORIES:**

**You already have a business and you're searching for ways to rapidly grow it online.**

**Or you're a first time entrepreneur looking for ways to get an online business up and running quickly!**

**Regardless, you're in the right place! This book is designed to show you a beginner-friendly way to leverage the power of social media.**

WAIT! BEFORE YOU CONTINUE...

# Download the interactive mobile app!

**Scan QR codes throughout the book to access exclusive content and free bonus gifts from Blake!**

Make your experience interactive with the Social Profit Machine App! This book contains dozens of videos, bonus gifts, and useful resources from Blake that will help you start or grow your business online! **Just search "Social Profit Machine" in your app store to find it!**

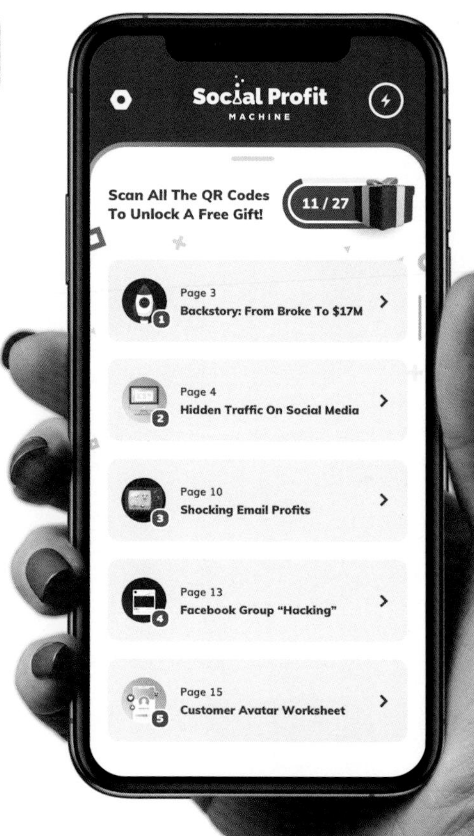


**Tip: There are 3 types of interactive content you'll find through the book:**

13 Value Videos

8 Free Bonus Gifts

6 Useful Websites

# Table of Contents

# The Hidden Opportunity On Social Media

# WARNING

**What if I told you there was a simple way to start or grow an online business that you didn't even know existed...**

and that with each passing second, you were missing out on HUGE opportunities to earn an income online with social media?

# My name is Blake Nubar.

**I'm a digital marketing, sales funnel, and lead generation expert. I've made millions online with my own products & services...**

And I'm about to show you a BRAND NEW way to "hack" your social media profiles to generate customers for any type of business online.

It doesn't require any special skills, and it doesn't involve running complicated ads.

**FROM BROKE TO MILLIONS**

Check out my backstory to see how I went from struggling & broke to earning millions online!

**VALUE VIDEO**

# In fact,

What I'm about to show you is probably

**THE EASIEST, FASTEST, & MOST BEGINNER-FRIENDLY WAY**

**TO GROW YOUR BUSINESS WITH SOCIAL MEDIA TODAY.**

And I'm willing to bet you didn't even know it existed!

# The hidden opportunity on Facebook™

## Let me explain.

Have you ever been scrolling around on Facebook™ when a post or comment catches your eye? And for whatever reason...

**you decide to click to view that person's profile page.**

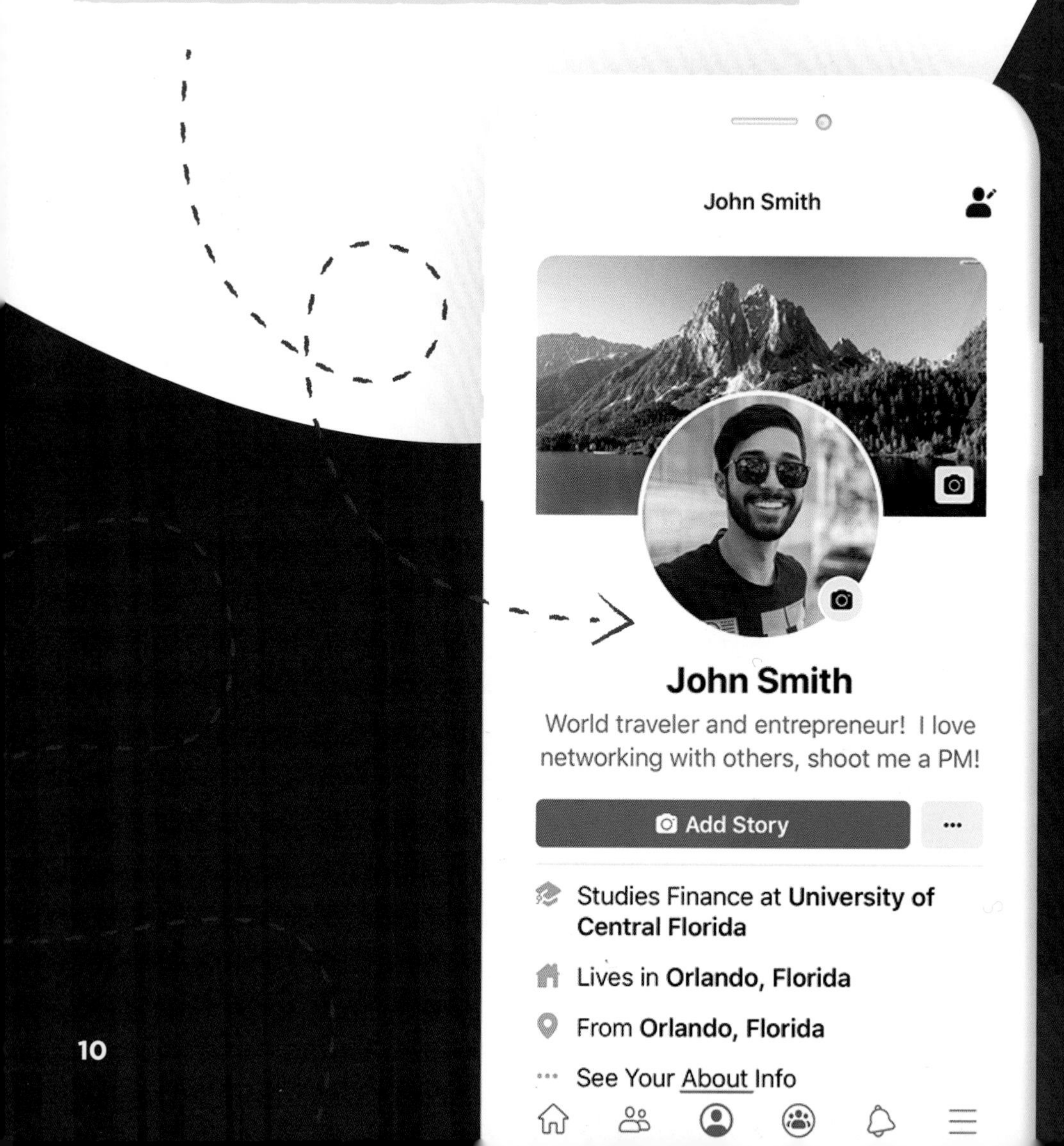

**HIDDEN SOCIAL MEDIA TRAFFIC**

You won't believe how many people do this to YOU every single day.

# If you've done that before, you're not alone. I do this all the time.

I'll see a post, or a comment, or a like that catches my eye, and I can't help but click to their profile page to see who that person is and what they're all about!

**3D PROFILE ANIMATION**

Watch how your profile can transform with this epic animation. If a picture is worth 1,000 words, this is worth a million!

VALUE VIDEO

# Let's be honest. We're all nosy on social media.

Have you ever wondered how often this is happening to you? How many people are clicking to view YOUR profile on a daily basis?

# So I decided to run an experiment...

where I treated my profile like a "landing page". I added buttons, links, and call-to-actions to my products & services in all the right places...

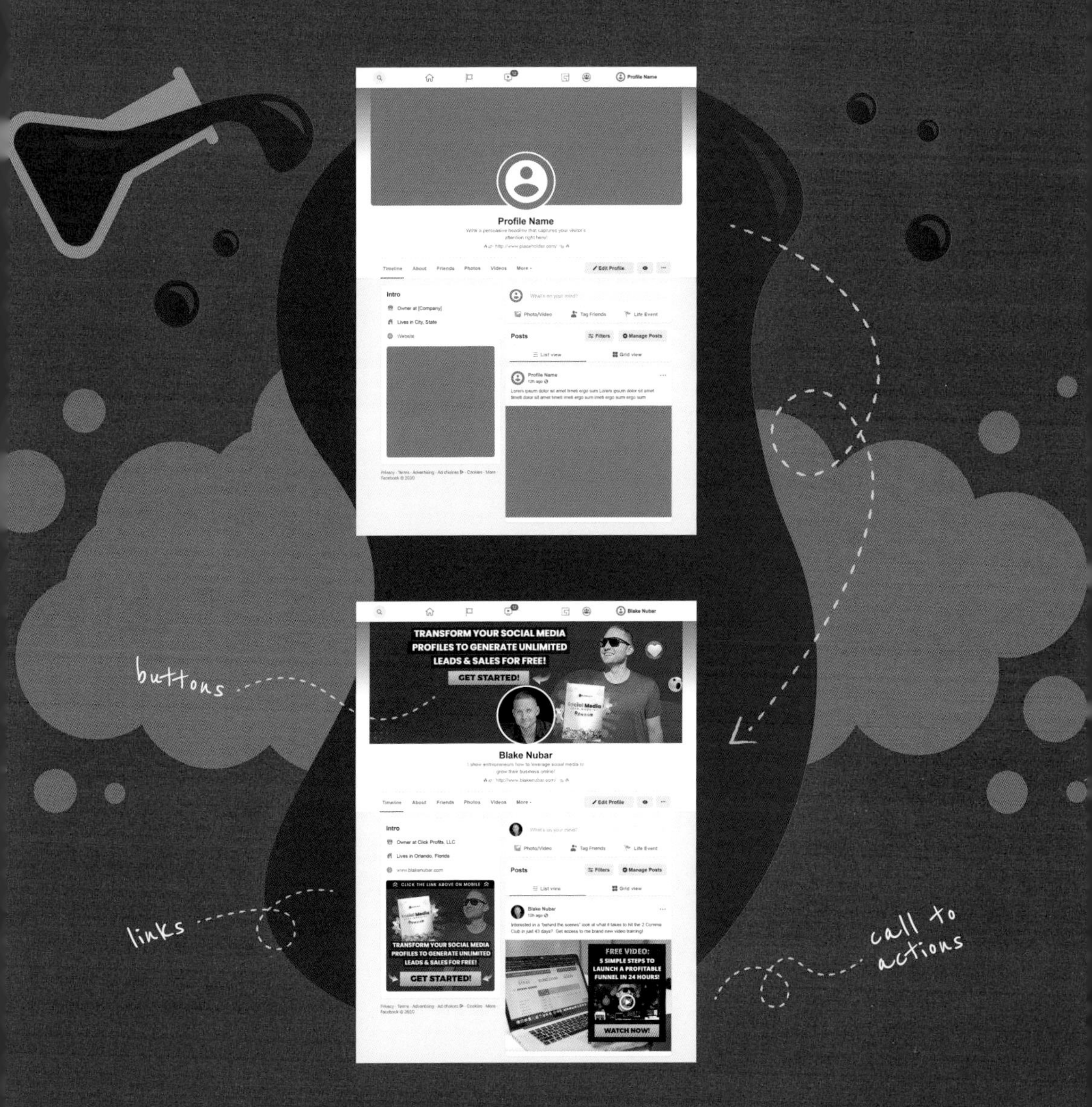


# and it worked like magic!

Once I was done, my profile had completely transformed into a landing page and I started getting results instantly! Without realizing it, I had tapped into a consistent stream of free traffic for my business, just by making a few simple tweaks to my Facebook™ profile!

## The moral of the story:

**EVEN THOUGH YOU CAN'T SEE THEM...**

# People are looking at your profile!

Every time you interact on social media - liking, commenting, sharing, posting - it generates an invisible crowd of "profile visitors," and every single one is a chance to grow your business!

Even if you're not that "active" on social media, you still have a natural flow of potential customers passing by your profile every single day.

## And if your profile isn't set up and optimized to capture those potential customers, you're missing out big time.

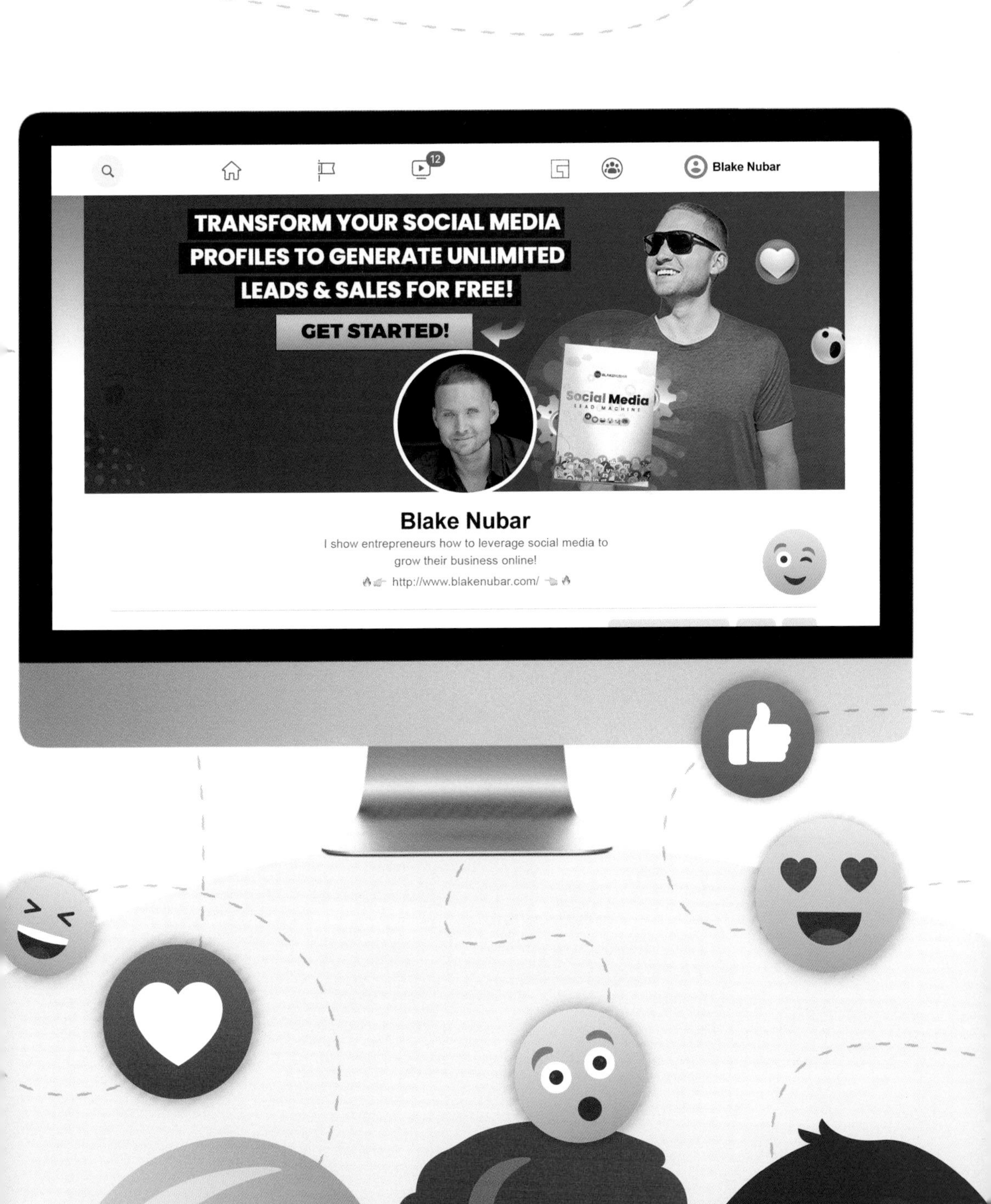
Blake Nubar
TRANSFORM YOUR SOCIAL MEDIA PROFILES TO GENERATE UNLIMITED LEADS & SALES FOR FREE!
GET STARTED!
Social Media
LEAD MACHINE
Blake Nubar
I show entrepreneurs how to leverage social media to grow their business online!
http://www.blakenubar.com/

**In this book, I'm going to show you how to completely transform your Facebook™ profile into a leads & sales machine that can help you get new customers for any type of business!**

1

Interact on social media (you can do it from your smartphone!)

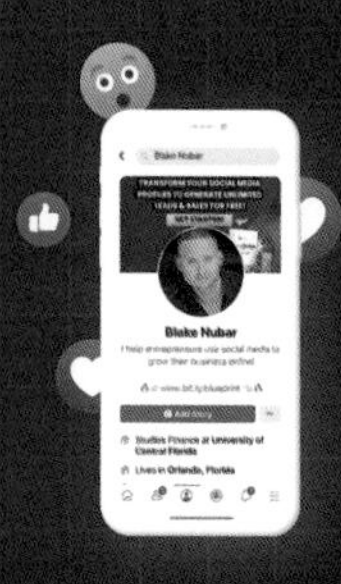

Transform your profile into a "landing page" that offers visitors an irresistible, free offer

Link your profile to a simple landing page where visitors enter their email to claim your irresistible freebie

Deliver on your promise by sending the free offer and inviting your visitors to your paid products & services

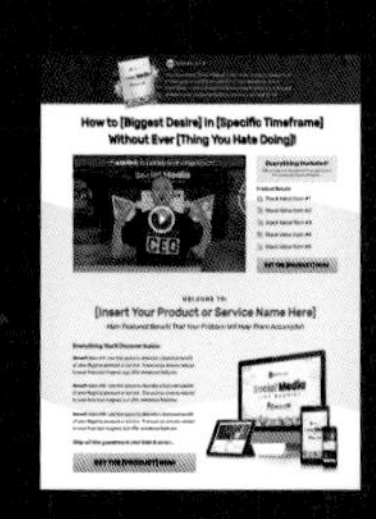

Ascend your visitors to your paid products & services and you generate income on auto-pilot, just by interacting on social media!

AT THIS POINT, YOU MIGHT BE THINKING

# Does this strategy actually work?

VALUE VIDEO
SEE JAW-DROPPING RESULTS
Hear from entrepreneurs just like you who have grown their businesses online!

# Entrepreneurs just like you are getting insane results with this system!

"I have never, in my 2 year entrepreneurial journey, **bought a course with so much value!"**

- DEVON W.

"I struggled to actually launch something prior to this. **Now I have new leads coming in every day."**

- CAMERON B.

**"Easily the best course I've ever taken in my life!** It only took me 2 days to set up my funnel...and it actually works!"

- COREY G.

**"This course is jam-packed with value.** Cuts straight to the point, no fluff, just how I like it."

- DANIEL S.

"I've been taking courses for 2 years and have gotten nothing done. But in this course, **I launched my funnel in 2 days!"**

- DEBORAH M.

**"Blake walks you through every single step** and makes everything incredibly simple to follow.

- JOE K.

"I'm getting **SO many leads** and building my email list SO quickly. I absolutely love how simple this program is!"

- GINTARE K.

"Within the first week of putting this up on my Facebook profile, **I immediately started generating leads organically."**

- JENNIFER D.

**"This is a phenomenal product.** It's been very instrumental in growing my business."

- JAREM A.

"It's **so easy to follow** it's actually ridiculous. I'm asking my 6 year old to go through the videos...it's that easy!"

- KLASS O.

"This is the **easiest money I've ever spent in my LIFE!** It doesn't get any easier than this."

- ALAN D.

"If you don't have this yet, you're missing out on something really great. **It has helped my business tremendously!"**

- JOE S.

"I can personally vouch that once you set this up you'll start getting **free leads on auto-pilot."**

- CRAIG E.

**"This program was absolutely incredible.** Thank you for being so generous and putting this all together!"

- MARK C.

"I totally needed this kick in the butt and I've learned a ton from this awesome program. **I already have 38 people in my course!"**

- MAXIME W.

"I can't make this up! Right after I launched this, **I added 60 new people to my program.** SIXTY new people! That's insane!"

- NICHOLAS D.

"This is the **best money I've ever spent!** It was extremely well put together and helped me take action!"

- SEAN F.

**"The impact on my life has been tremendous.** If you get an opportunity to take this course, I suggest you take it."

- LARRY P.

"This is probably the best course I've ever taken. In a few simple steps you're getting **FREE leads from social media."**

- MIODRAG M.

**"This gave me clarity and precision** on how to position myself and helped me launch a new service!

- LYNDON S.

"He really opens up and shows you everything you need to build a funnel and **generate new leads for your business."**

- SABRINA W.

"When we launched the funnel, we had **300 new people take our offer immediately,** and another 150 in the next few days."

- AI R.

"This was a **super awesome course** that allowed me to launch my funnel QUICKLY."

- BRENDA M.

"As always, **Blake has OVER delivered** and gives you all the tools to get this up and running perfectly."

- KALLAN D.

"This is a great program! Very intuitive, **step-by-step content that gets results quickly!"**

- MIKE M.

# Reasons to set this up today

### It's brand new!

Barely anyone is doing this which means it's easy to get results quickly!

### Beginner friendly

It requires no special skills to set this up (no techy stuff here).

### Generate leads & sales

Unlock a new stream of leads & sales for your new or existing business.

### Works in every niche imaginable

This works the exact same for any type of business in every niche imaginable.

### Set it & forget it

Once you set it up, it becomes a completely passive source of income.

### Quick setup!

This doesn't take weeks or months to do...you can set it all up TODAY!

Your ideas
Use this page to jot down
any ideas or inspiration!

# Notes

# The 8 Step Formula

1

Choose a path for your online biz

2

Create your lead magnet

3

Write a persuasive call to action

4

Optimize your Facebook™ profile

5

Launch an effective landing page

6

Add in follow-up emails

7

Engage on social media

8

Get unlimited leads & sales!

Finish!

STEP 1

# Choose a path for your online biz.

# Choose your path.

**Before we get down to the nitty gritty, let's determine which path you're on with your online business.**

You already have your own product or service that you want to set this system up for.

2

You're starting from scratch and need to figure out what you want to promote to start earning online.

**The next couple pages will be dedicated to showing what to do if you fall into category 2 - you're starting from scratch and need to find a product to promote.**

**If you already have your product or service, feel free to skip ahead to step 2 found on page 32 of this blueprint.**

# Affiliate marketing

**Unless you plan on spending an exorbitant amount of time & energy building your own product or service over the coming weeks, I believe your fastest path to launching an online business with the Social Profit Machine is affiliate marketing.**

Affiliate marketing gives you the opportunity to promote OTHER people's products and start earning commissions instantly (so you don't have to spend a crazy amount of time building your own).

## HOW AFFILIATE MARKETING WORKS

Choose an affiliate product you want to promote and sign up to get your unique link

Visitors click on your unique link and are sent to the merchant's sales page

Visitor buys the product you're promoting

You earn 50%-80% commissions on sales!

**HOW AFFILIATE MARKETING WORKS**

Blake will break it down in a simple way so it's easy to understand!

# How to find a product

**Visit clickbank.com**

ClickBank is a popular affiliate platform that allows internet entrepreneurs just like you to promote OTHER people's products so you can get your online business off the ground quickly!

In the left column of their website, you'll see TONS of products available in every niche imaginable that you can promote instantly to earn HUGE commissions!

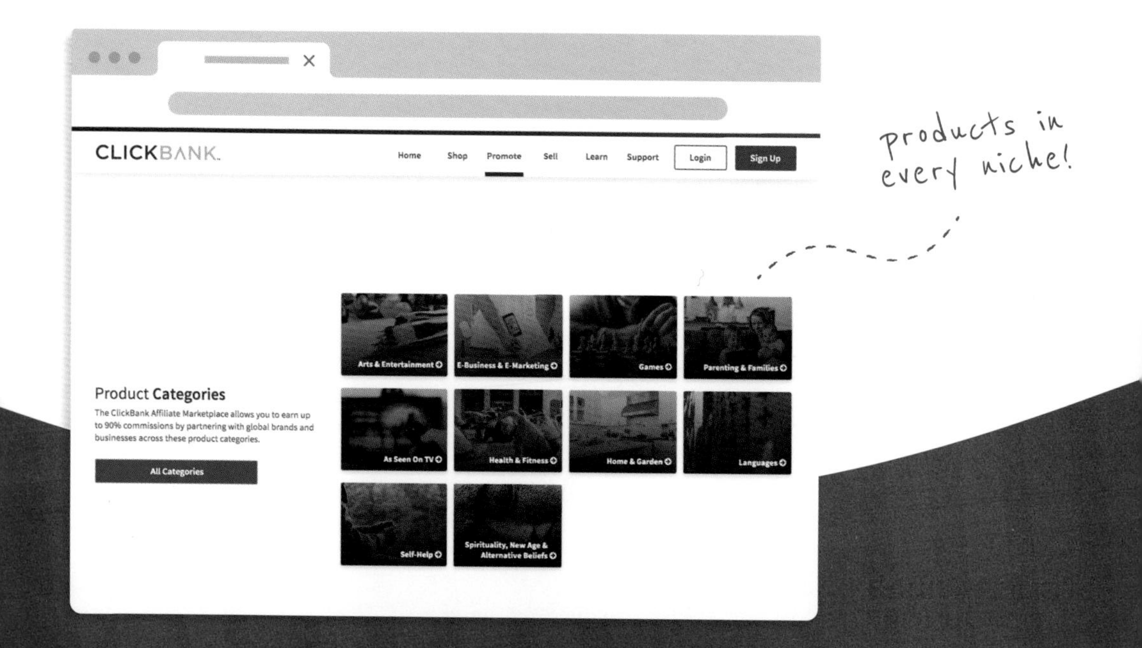


**Take a couple minutes to browse through the products they have available, find one that suits your interests, and sign up to get your affiliate link. You'll need it for the next steps of this book!**

# Need help nailing down your niche?

At the end of the day, choosing a niche comes down to one important question: "Who is your ideal customer who you feel most comfortable serving?"

I created this worksheet to help you figure out who your IDEAL customer is online. After browsing through ClickBank's affiliate product options, print out this worksheet to help you think through the exact type of customer you would want to work with.

**Customer Avatar Worksheet**

CREATED FOR:

(What is the target business/product?)

**Quote:**
(Statement that sums up your avatar's feelings related to the challenge/goal most closely related to your business/product)

**Avatar Background**
Name:
Age:
Gender:
Location:
Marital status:
Occupation/job title:
Level of education:
Annual income:

**Messaging**
How will you position your business/product to help solve the avatar's challenges and/or achieve their goals?

**A Day in the Life**
Describe what a typical day looks like for your avatar

**Make Life Easier**
What would make your avatar's life easier? List things that are relevant to your business/product

**Sources of Information**
Books/magazines:
Blogs/websites:
Influencers:
Brand affinities:
Other:

**Content Preferences**
Media choice:
Go-to sources:
Favorite social media platforms:
Least favorite social media platforms:

**Triggers and Objections**
Why would your avatar buy from you and what would keep them from buying?
Triggers:
Objections:

**Challenges and Pain Points**
What are the negative or unpleasant things that your avatar is moving away from?
Challenges:
Pain points:

**Goals and Values**
What does your avatar want and how do their values affect the things they want?
Goals:
Values:

**Before Experience**
Detail the avatar's experience before interacting with your business/product. What does your avatar have right now that they don't want? How does that make them feel?

**After Experience**
Detail the avatar's experience after interacting with your business/product. What desirable thing(s) has your avatar gained? How does that make them feel?

CUSTOMER AVATAR WORKSHEET
Download this customer avatar worksheet to help nail down your niche!
BONUS GIFT

Your ideas
Use this page to jot down
any ideas or inspiration!

# Notes

# The 8 Step Formula

Choose a path for your online biz

Create your lead magnet

Write a persuasive call to action

Optimize your Facebook™ profile

Launch an effective landing page

Add in follow-up emails

Engage on social media

Get unlimited free leads & sales!

Finish!

STEP 2

# Create your "lead magnet"

# Offer profile visitors a gift, AKA a "lead magnet."

**The best way to get your profile visitors to take action on your products & services is to offer them something of value for free up front.**

The goal is to offer your visitor a free lead magnet on your profile in exchange for their email address. Make sure what you're offering is irresistible!

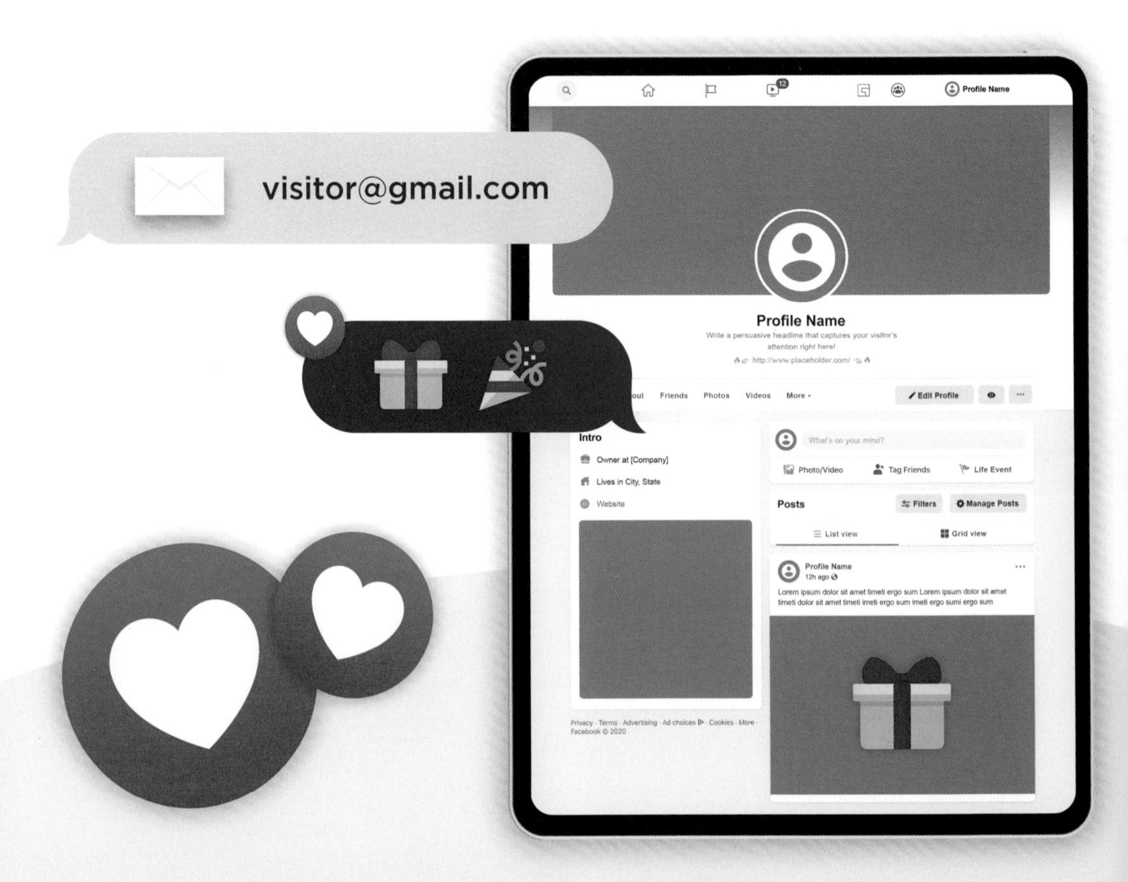

# Proven lead magnet ideas

**Here's a list of lead magnet concepts that are proven to be effective at enticing visitors to take action:**

 Mini course

 Infographics

 Case study

 Ebook

 Checklist

 Swipe file

 Toolkit

 Newsletter

 Quiz

 Video

 Podcast episode

 PowerPoint

 Giveaway

 Template

 Discount

# Proven lead magnet ideas

If you don't want to create your own lead magnet from scratch, I recommend visiting The PLR Store!

They have an endless variety of inexpensive freebies that you can purchase and start using right out of the box.

**Visit theplrstore.com**

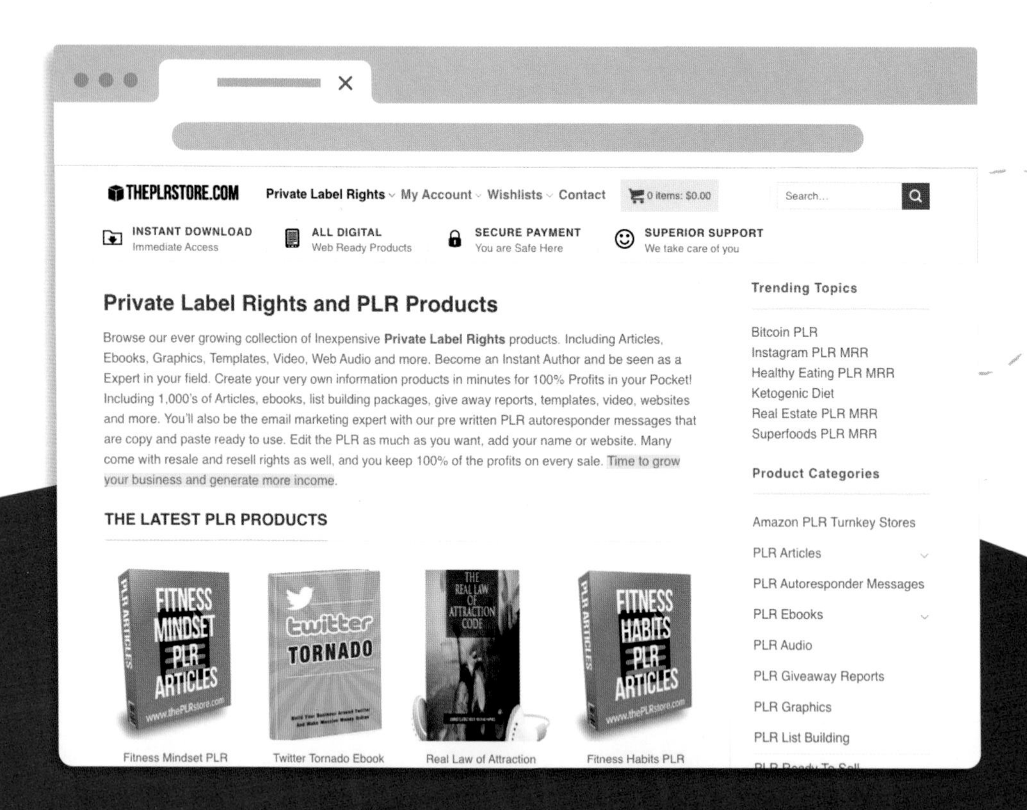

USEFUL WEBSITE

**PLR STORE LEAD MAGNETS**

Browse through the SUPER affordable, done-for-you lead magnets available in the PLR Store!

# Presenting your lead magnet

## We're all visual creatures.  

So it helps to present your lead magnet in a "mockup". This often takes the form of a box, book, coupon, etc.

Although it's just a graphic, this gives the impression of tangible value and increases the chances that a visitor will want to take action to get their hands on it.

BONUS GIFT
LEAD MAGNET PSD TEMPLATES
I created these epic lead magnet photoshop templates to make it easy for you to get a stunning result quickly!
YOUR LOGO
[Insert Your]
Product Name
COUPON
[Insert Your Product Name]
Lorem Ipsum Sit Amet

# How to find the perfect mockup for your lead magnet

Here's some inspiration below to help get your creative juices flowing. If you're interested in a wider variety of templates, I highly recommend visiting www.graphicriver.net. They have an incredible selection of cheap graphics - you're bound to find the perfect one!

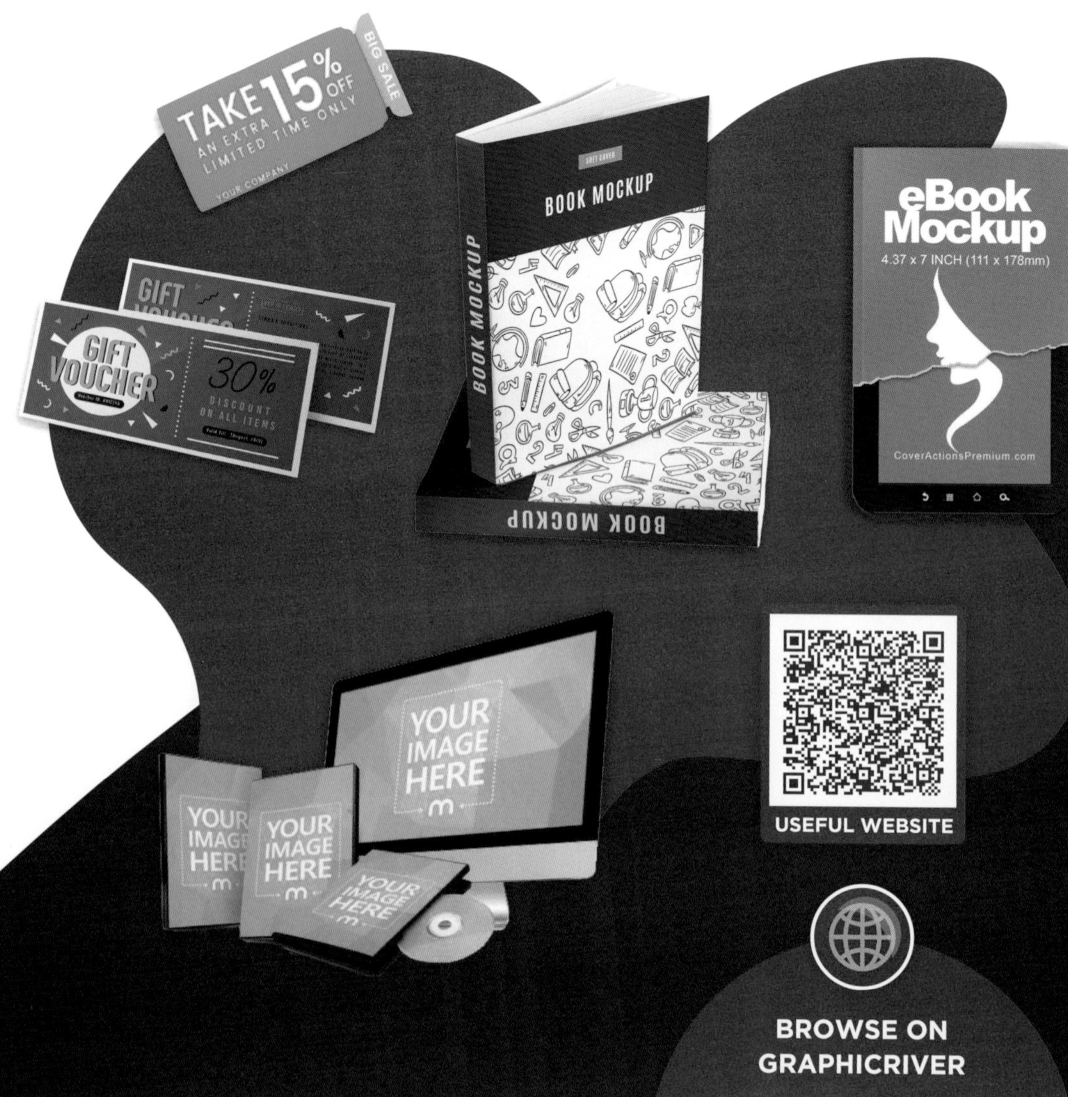


**BROWSE ON GRAPHICRIVER**

For endless inspiration, visit www.graphicriver.net and search keywords related to your business!

## OUTSOURCING MADE EASY

Visit Fiverr to hire an affordable designer to create your lead magnet mockup.

# Get your mockup fast and cheap!

USEFUL WEBSITE

If you're a busy business owner and want an easy way to get a mockup created for your lead magnet...

**Head over to fiverr.com and give them this design brief.**

This is a very inexpensive service that any graphic designer can turn around for you quickly.

## Lead Magnet Mockup

**JOB BRIEF**

**Hi there!**

I'm looking for someone to design a box mockup for my new lead magnet. The title of the resource is called **"[insert your title here]".**

The information contained inside is designed to help **[target market]** accomplish **[goal].**

**Here are some visual references of the style I'm going for.**

As a final deliverable, could you please send me a PNG of the mockup (with transparent background). Please optimize the file using http://optimizilla.com before sending!

Let me know if you want to take on the project and estimated turnaround time!

Thank you!

**[Your Name]**

BONUS GIFT

## JOB BRIEF EXAMPLE

Download this simple job brief to let your designer know exactly what you want for your mockup!

# Your ideas

Use this page to jot down
any ideas or inspiration!

# Notes

# The 8 Step Formula

Choose a path for your online biz

Create your lead magnet

Write a persuasive call to action

Optimize your Facebook™ profile

Launch an effective landing page

Add in follow-up emails

Engage on social media

Get unlimited leads & sales!

Finish!

STEP 3

# Write a persuasive call to action.

Learn how

# Write your call to action.

**Now it's time to write your lead magnet's "call to action" that prompts profile visitors to take action.**

What we create in this step of the formula will placed in the "intro" section of your Facebook™ profile.

A large percentage of clicks on your profile will come from this section, so we'll want to use every possible advantage to draw attention to it.

**Here's a diagram of the elements we'll need to create a captivating call to action:**

LET'S START BY WRITING A COMPELLING

# Headline

## 70% of your visitors will make a decision to take action based on your headline alone!

Most often, it's best to craft a headline that presents your lead magnet in a clear, concise, benefit-oriented way.

Write Your Persuasive
Lead Magnet Headline!
your link goes here

# My favorite headline formula

If you're stuck on figuring out what your headline should be, below is one of my favorite templates I always recommend (and still use myself)!

How to [biggest desire] in [specific time frame] without [thing you hate doing]!

**MY FAVORITE HEADLINE TEMPLATE**

Download an editable version of my favorite headline template and fill in the blanks to create your own!

CHOOSE AN EYE-CATCHING

# Relevant emoji

The fingers pointing in towards your link universally apply, but you'll want to add a second emoji next to it that's related to your business. It's subtle, but even a tiny graphic that specifically resonates with your audience will draw attention and drive more people to take your lead magnet.

**For example, if a local winery in San Jose, CA wants to get more customers in to visit their location, they could use a wine glass emoji to catch the attention of profile visitors who enjoy wine.**

# Choose your emoji!

There are TONS of emojis you can choose from!

You're bound to find the perfect one that matches your free lead magnet!

**BROWSE EMOJI OPTIONS**

Check out the HUGE number of different emojis that you can choose from for your call to action!

USEFUL WEBSITE

ADD IN YOUR

# Landing page link

Now it's time to add the link to your landing page, website, or sales funnel! This is where visitors will actually land to claim your free lead magnet.

Write Your Persuasive
Lead Magnet Headline!
your link goes here
VALUE VIDEO

**HOW LINK TRACKERS WORK**

Learn about useful software that helps you track "link click activity" on your profile!

**HEADLINE BRAINSTORMING WORKSHEET**

Use this worksheet to brainstorm different headline ideas for your lead magnet!

# Headline Worksheet

Use the lines below to experiment with your best headline ideas before you move on to the next step of the book!

1

2

3

4

5

6

7

8

9

10

11

12

13

14

15

16

17

18

Done!
Keep this handy.
We'll be using this in the next steps
to optimize your profile!

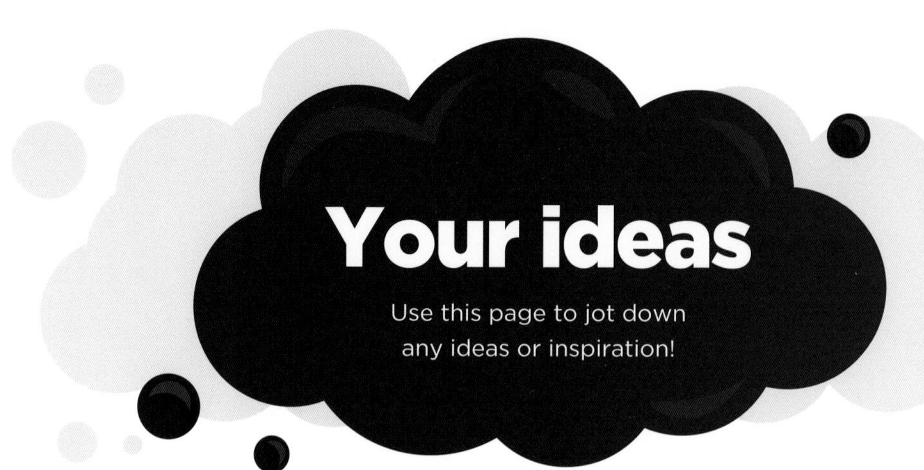
Your ideas
Use this page to jot down
any ideas or inspiration!

# Notes

# The 8 Step Formula

Choose a path for your online biz

Create your lead magnet

Write a persuasive call to action

4

Optimize your Facebook™ profile

5

Launch an effective landing page

6

Add in follow-up emails

7

Engage on social media

8

Get unlimited leads & sales!

Finish!

STEP 4

# Optimize your Facebook™ profile.

# Introduction to the Facebook™ profile

Facebook™ gives everyone the ability to customize their profile to use as a tool to interact with other members on the platform. I'm gong to show you creative ways to leverage it in a way that establishes you as an authority in your industry.

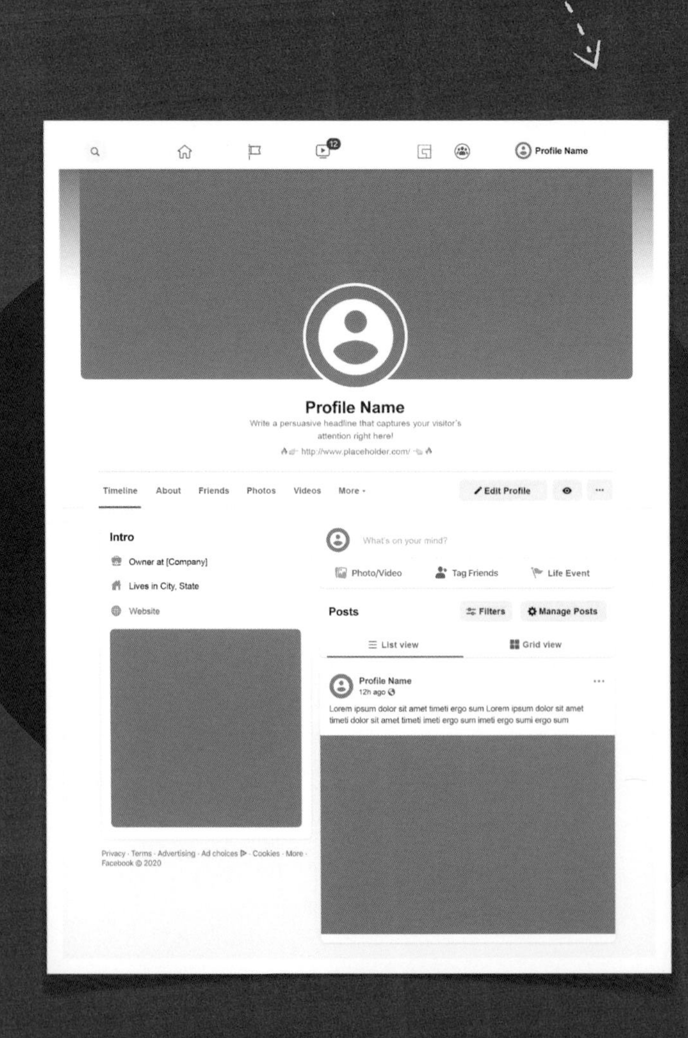

# It's time to turn your profile into a powerful lead trap!

## If you had to guess...

Which one of these profiles do you think converts visitors into customers better than the other?

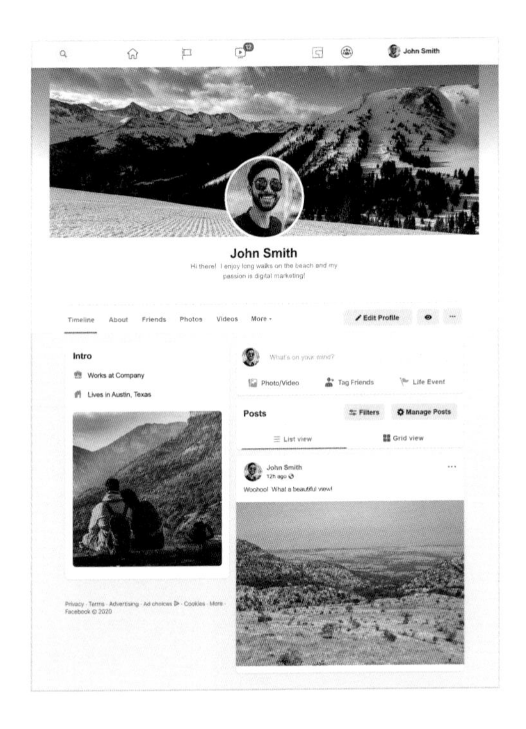


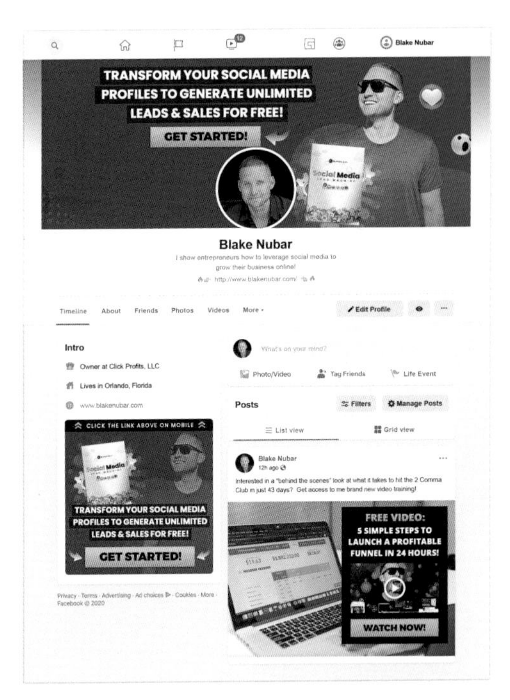


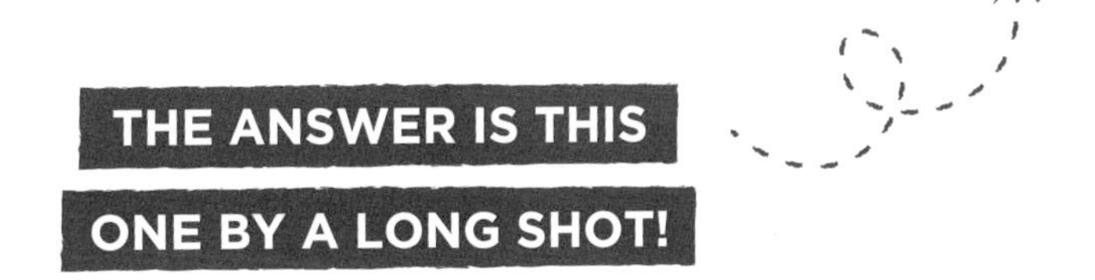

THE ANSWER IS THIS
ONE BY A LONG SHOT!

# How To Optimize Your Facebook™ Profile

**There are 5 different strategies you can use to optimize your profile.**

When all combined together, your profile becomes a powerful "sales funnel" that captures new customers for your online business.

**HOW TO OPTIMIZE YOUR PROFILE**

Let me show you exactly how this profile system works!

# ❶ Cover photo

Your cover photo is the "billboard" of your profile and is crucial in presenting your lead magnet.

The 3 key elements to include are your headline, button, and lead magnet mockup.

# Follow the layout specifications below to get the best possible result.

This is easy to do yourself, or just pass it on to your graphic assistant. Make sure to keep all important content inside of the yellow outline to make sure your cover is optimized for mobile viewing!

The yellow outline indicates the **"mobile safe area."** Keep all your important elements inside this area to make sure your cover is presented well to mobile visitors!

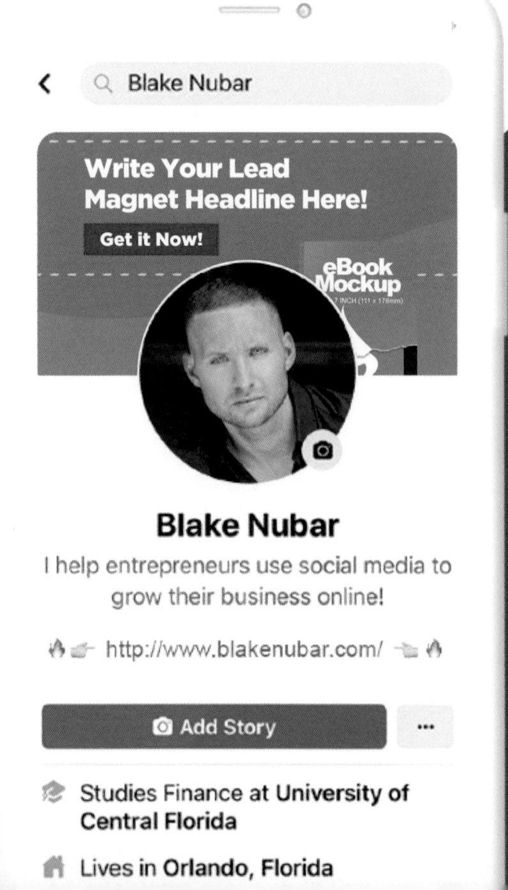


**IMPORTANT!**

Don't forget to check how your cover photo appears on your mobile device!

# Here's a quick diagram of how the cover photo works:

**1** Your headline, button, and lead magnet mockup will entice visitors to click.

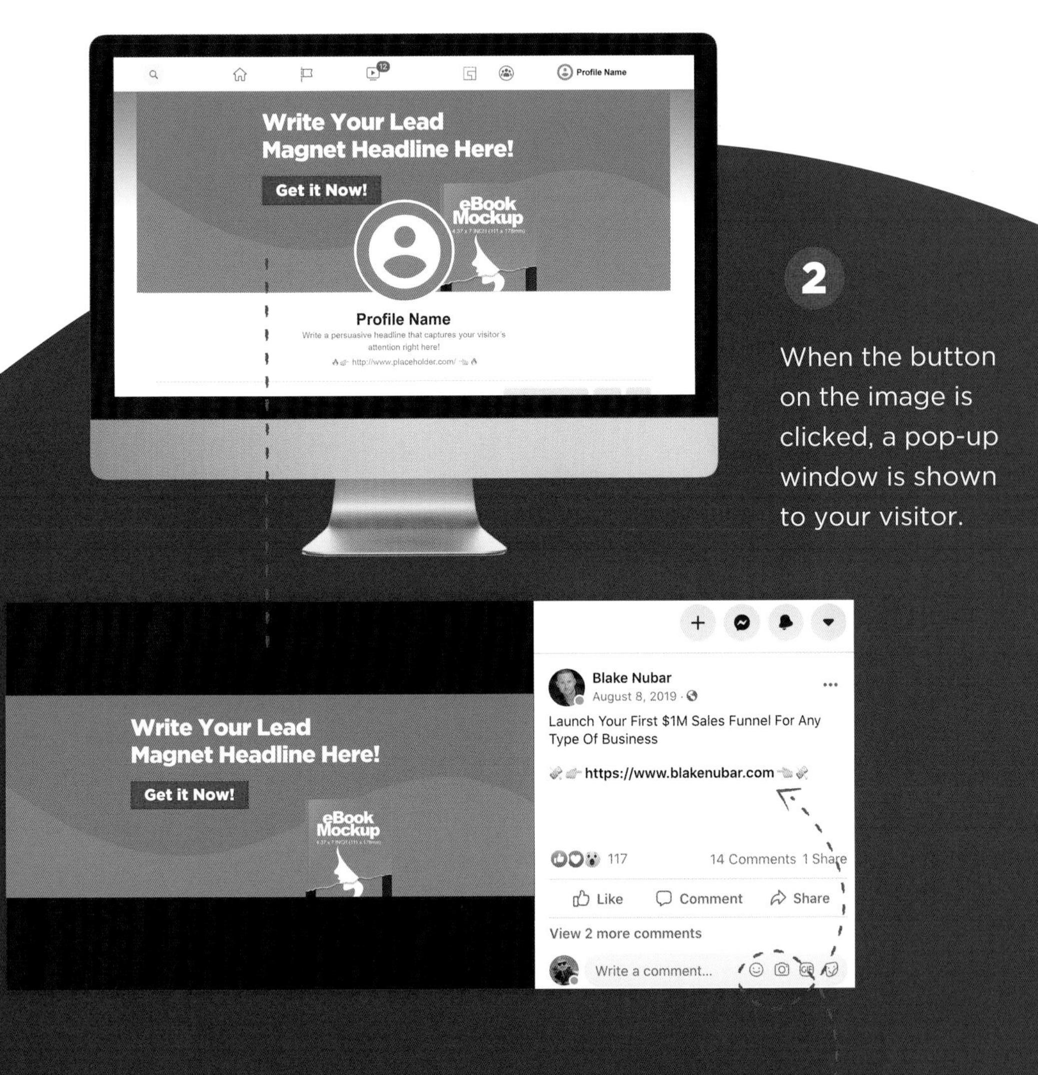


**2** When the button on the image is clicked, a pop-up window is shown to your visitor.

**3** Present the visitor with your "call to action" (from the previous section) to claim the free lead magnet.

# Cover photo examples

Here are some examples of cover photos that are proven and have worked incredibly well for me and entrepreneurs I work with!

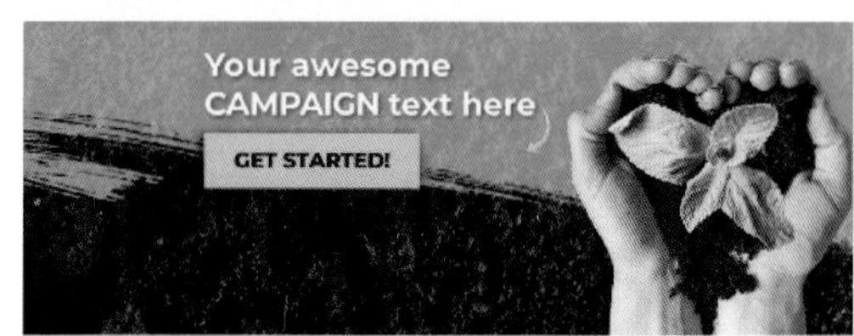

# 2 Profile photo

You may not realize it, but people click your profile photo all the time (like I mentioned earlier...we're all nosy)!

**So make sure your call to action is strategically placed on your profile photo pop-up as well.**

**ANIMATE YOUR PROFILE PIC**

Bring your profile to life with an eye-catching video created with this unique mobile app!

**VALUE VIDEO**

Present the visitor with your "call to action" (from the previous section) to claim the free lead magnet.

# 3 Intro section

The Intro Section is a key area of your profile that gives visitors an immediate opportunity to click your landing page link, so it's important to make sure it draws attention.

**All you have to do is copy your exact "call to action" from the previous section and paste it here!**

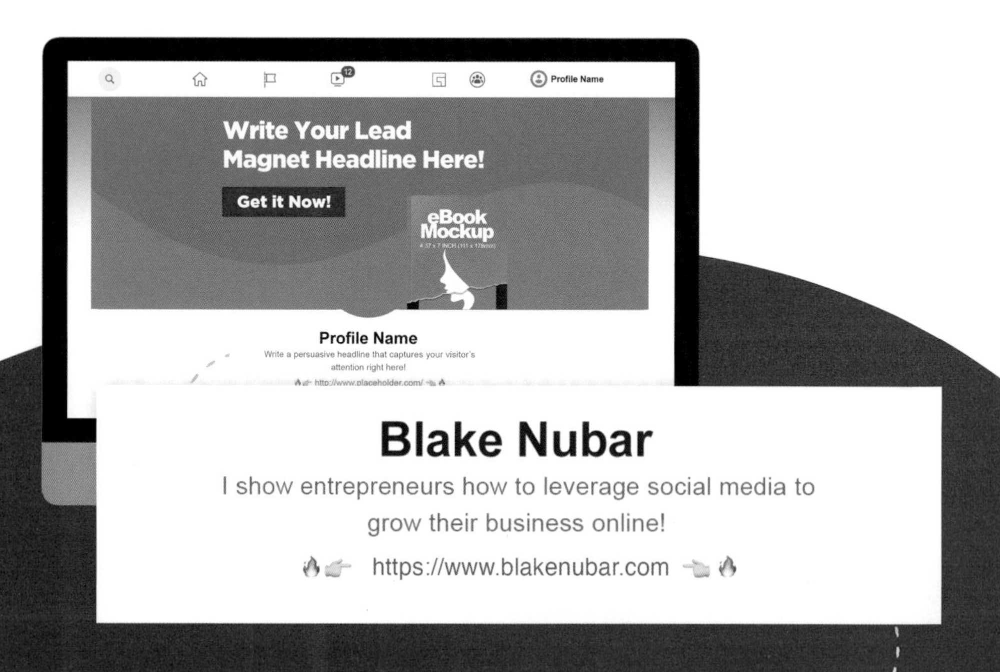
Profile Name
Write Your Lead Magnet Headline Here!
Get it Now!
eBook Mockup
Profile Name
Write a persuasive headline that captures your visitor's attention right here!
Blake Nubar
I show entrepreneurs how to leverage social media to grow their business online!
https://www.blakenubar.com

Present the visitor with your "call to action" (from the previous section) to claim the free lead magnet.

# 4 Bio link

The Bio Link is an obvious (yet often overlooked) area of your profile to add your landing page link. It's easy and quick to add your link here and give visitors another potential area to click to claim your lead magnet!

Add your link to your bio to give visitors another opportunity to click to your landing page.

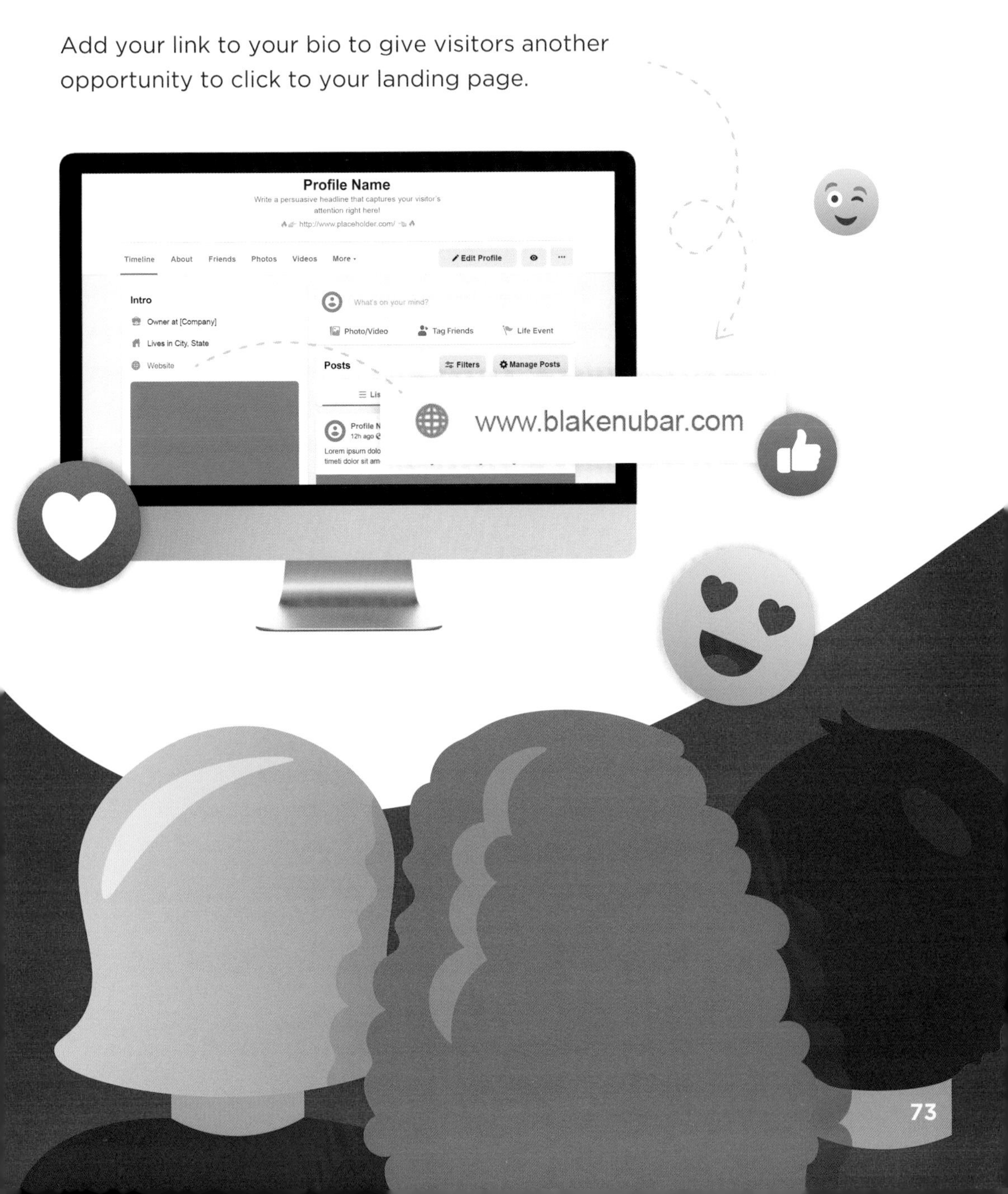

# 5 Featured photo

The featured photo is a "secret weapon" that I rarely see anyone utilize properly. Similar to your cover photo, there are 3 important elements to get the best results: headline, button, and mockup.

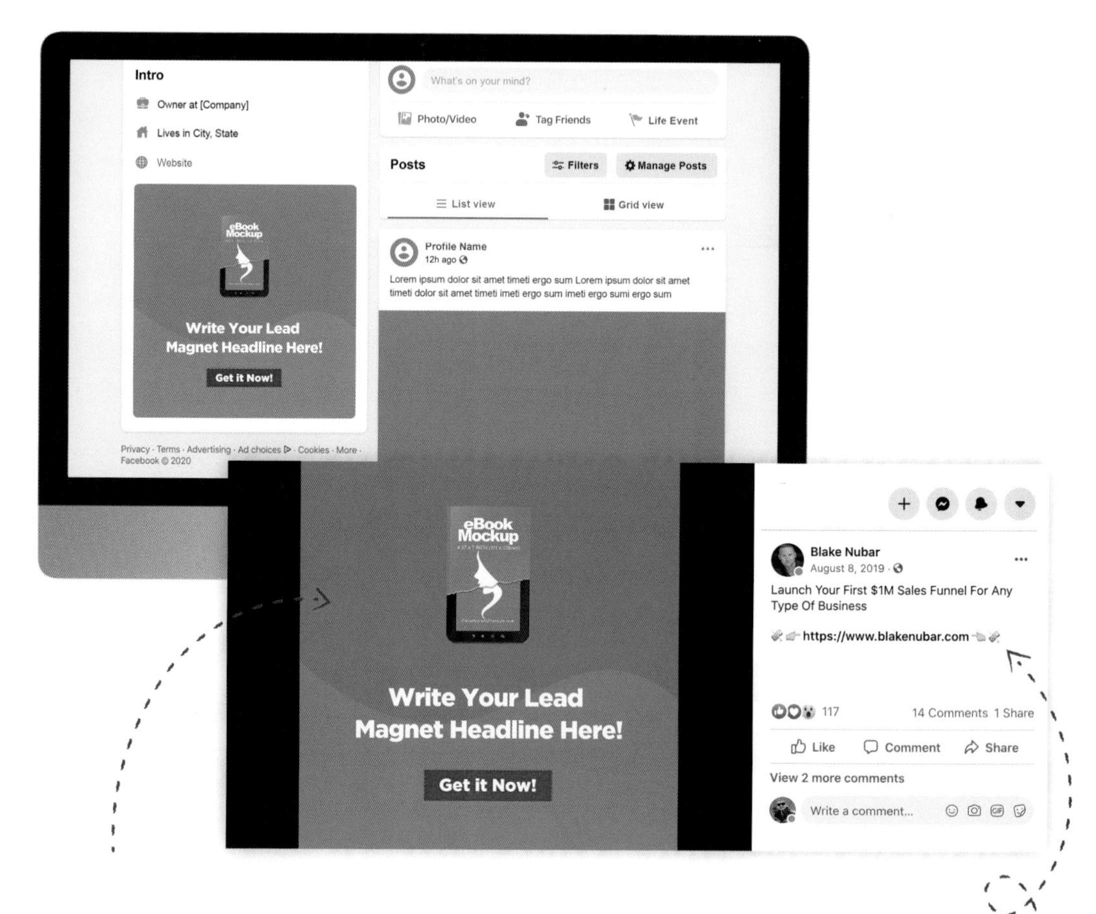


These 3 elements are critical to catching the eye of your visitor and getting them to take action! In this little "billboard" they can see that you have something valuable to offer and that they can get instant access to it.

In the pop-up window, present the visitor with your "call to action" (from the previous section) to claim the free lead magnet.

# Featured photo examples

Here are some examples of featured photos that are proven and have worked incredibly well for me and entrepreneurs I work with!

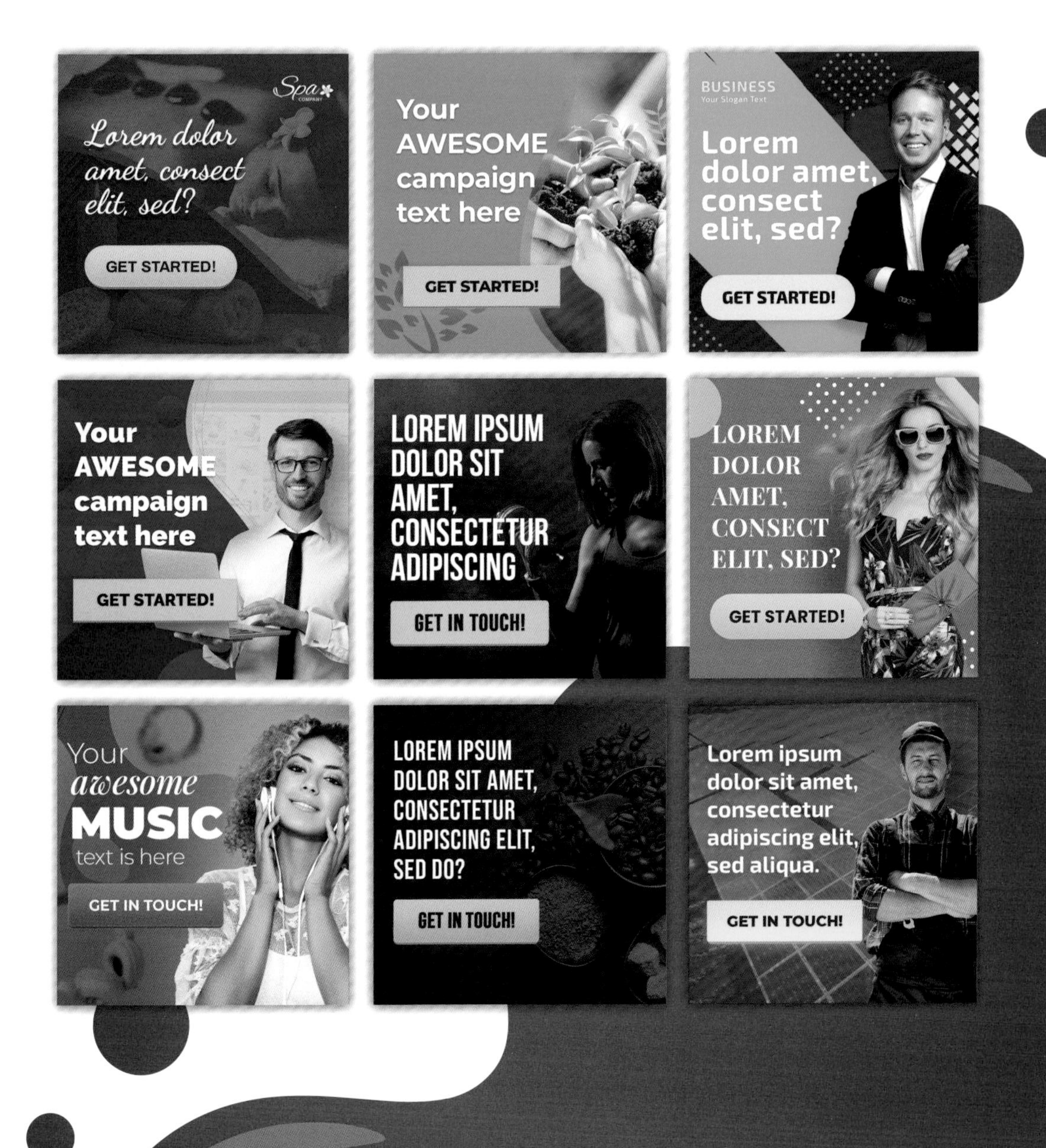

# Your profile is ready!

Once you've finished optimizing these 5 areas of your profile, it will be transformed into a powerful landing page that siphons free traffic from social media!

With this strategy, your profile is 100% optimized to capture as many profile visitors as possible and convert them into customers.

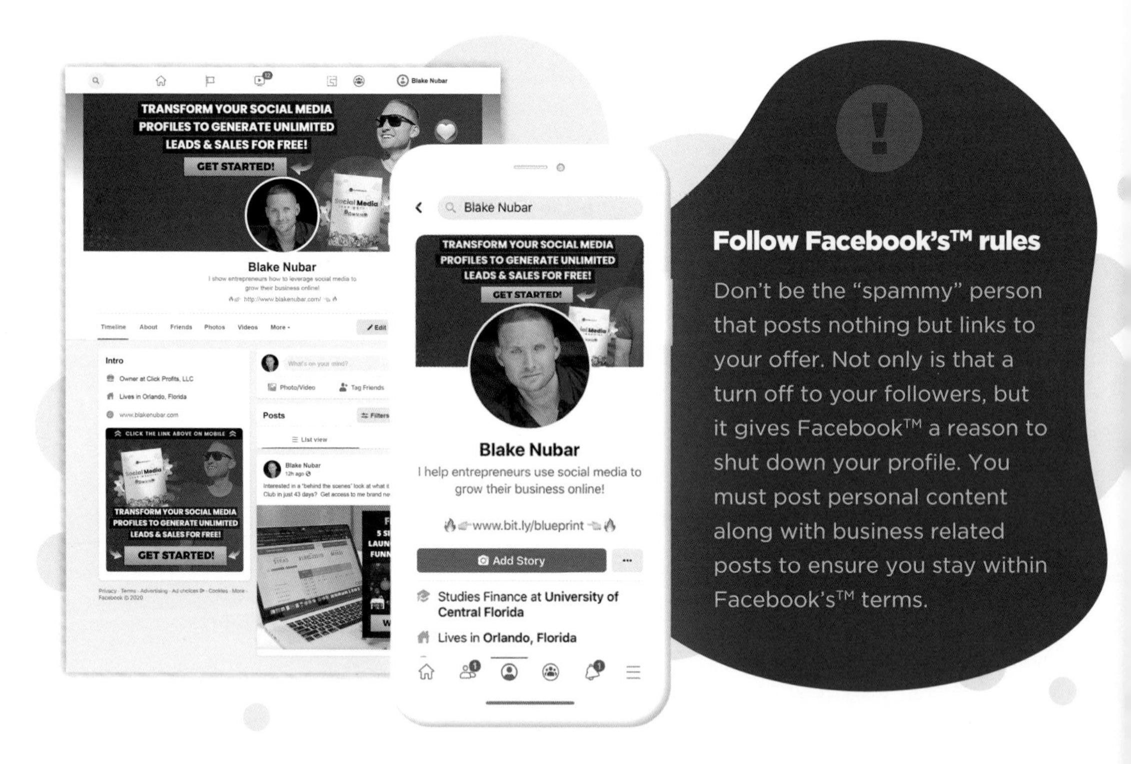


### Follow Facebook's™ rules

Don't be the "spammy" person that posts nothing but links to your offer. Not only is that a turn off to your followers, but it gives Facebook™ a reason to shut down your profile. You must post personal content along with business related posts to ensure you stay within Facebook's™ terms.

**In the next section, we'll show you how to send this "profile" traffic to a simple landing page that converts visitors into new leads for your business!**

# Business page

We also recommend setting up a Facebook™ Business Page! It works almost exactly the same way...but it has some additional features that make it extra powerful to grow your business!

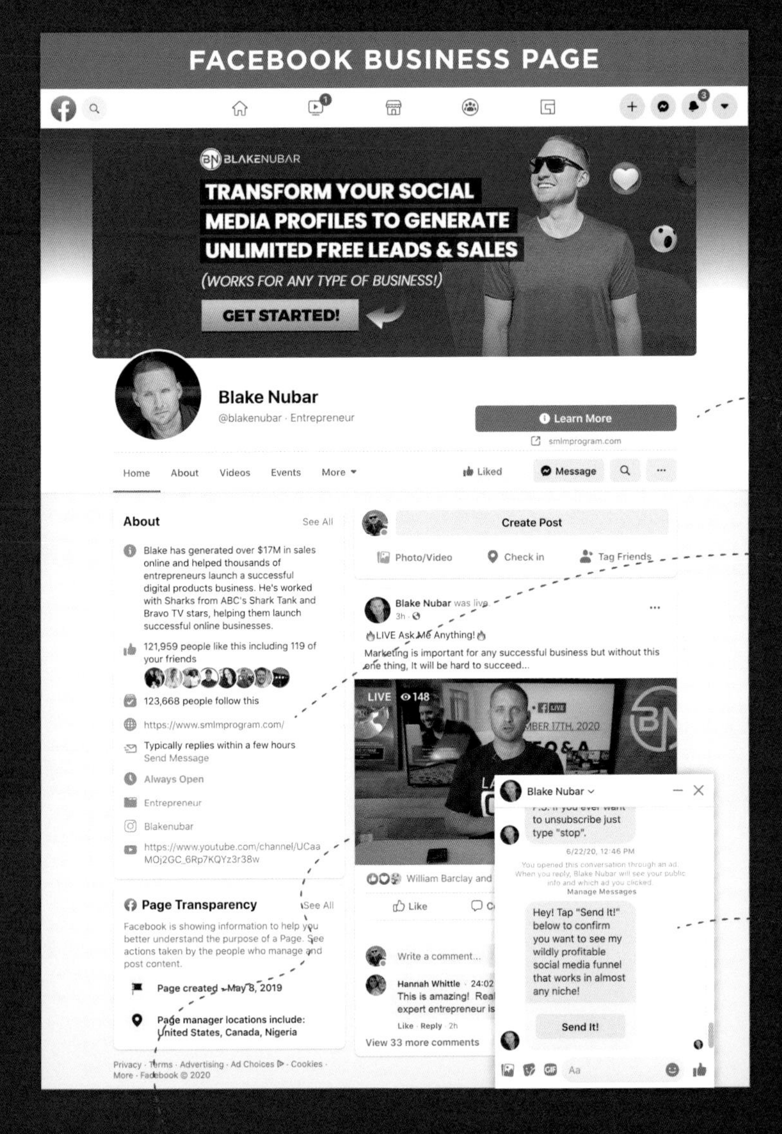


**Built-in button** that links straight to your products, services, or affiliate offers

**Enhanced "About" section** that enables native links to your funnel, landing page, and social media channels

**Facebook™ Lives** can be an especially powerful tool to draw eyeballs to your business page and drive traffic!

**Messenger bot** to interact with your visitors without having to lift a finger!

Your ideas
Use this page to jot down
any ideas or inspiration!

# Notes

# The 8 Step Formula

Choose a path for your online biz

Create your lead magnet

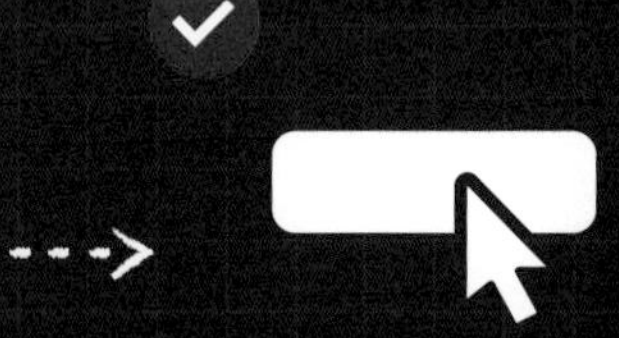

Write a persuasive call to action

Optimize your Facebook™ profile

5

Launch an effective landing

6

Add in follow-up emails

7

Engage on social media

8

Get unlimited leads & sales!

Finish!

STEP 5

# Launch an effective landing page

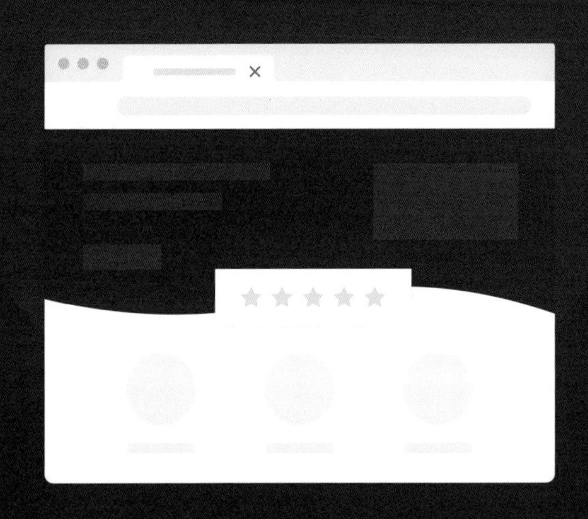

# Simple Landing Page

At this point, we've optimized your profile to get customers to take action on your free lead magnet...but we still need somewhere to send them so they can get access to it!

That's where this simple landing page comes into play. It's designed to quickly and easily allow visitors to input their email and claim the freebie you're offering.

**Here's the diagram to remind you how it works:**

Interact on social media (you can do it from your smartphone!)

Transform your profile into a "landing page" that offers visitors an irresistible, free offer

Link your profile to a simple landing page where visitors enter their email to claim your irresistible freebie.

Deliver on your promise by sending the free offer and invite the visitor to your paid products & services!

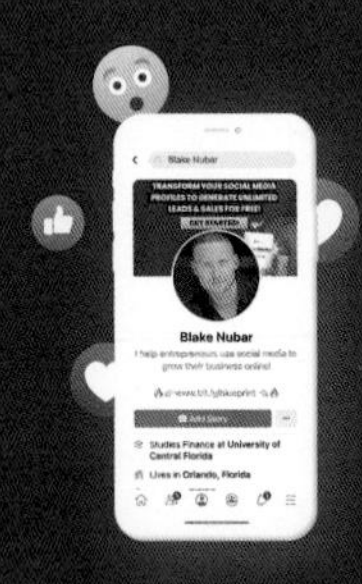

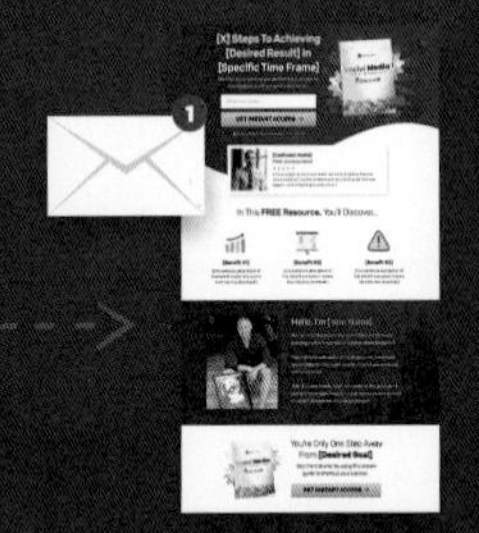

Ascend your visitors to your paid products & services and generate income on auto-pilot, just by interacting on social media!

# Always get the email!

**The main goal of this simple landing page is to give visitors access to your lead magnet in exchange for their email address.**

This step might be simple, but it's of paramount importance!

Once you have someone's email, you can market your products & services to them forever!

**You may have heard this before and it's 100% true no matter what type of business you're in - your email list is your goldmine.**

# Drag n' drop builders

**Now if you're thinking, "How do I get a landing page like that?!"**

Don't worry! With the tools available to us today, " I'm not a techy person" is no longer an excuse! If you're totally new to this stuff, know that every popular landing page builder out there today is designed with YOU in mind.

It's all drag and drop! All your options are easy to use and require no previous experience.

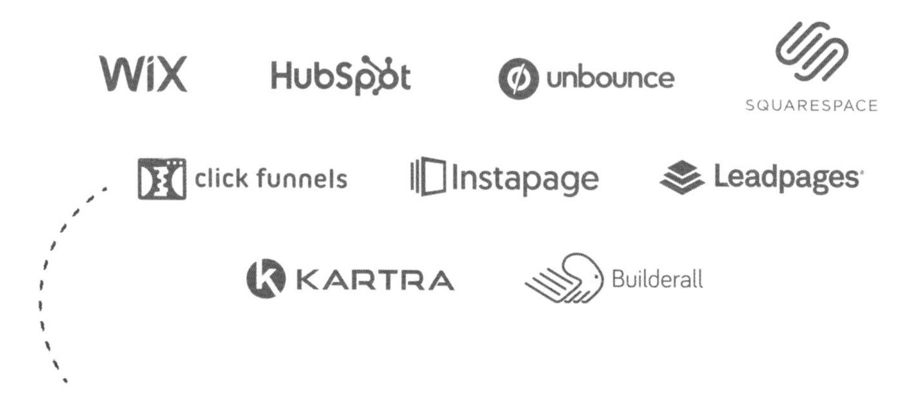


## ClickFunnels

My favorite option (and what we recommend to all our customers) is ClickFunnels! It's a simple, drag n' drop landing page builder that's designed for total beginners.

But, the choice is totally up to you! There's lots of great (and inexpensive) options out there. Check them out and use any that suit your specific needs!

USEFUL WEBSITE

**TRY CLICKFUNNELS TODAY**

Test drive the world's leading funnel building platform! It's perfect for beginners.

# Landing page

## Let's talk about what elements to include on your landing page

It's important to mirror the same information from your profile here on the landing page. Having "congruency" between them lets the visitor know they've landed in the right place and reinforces their desire to take action on your lead magnet.

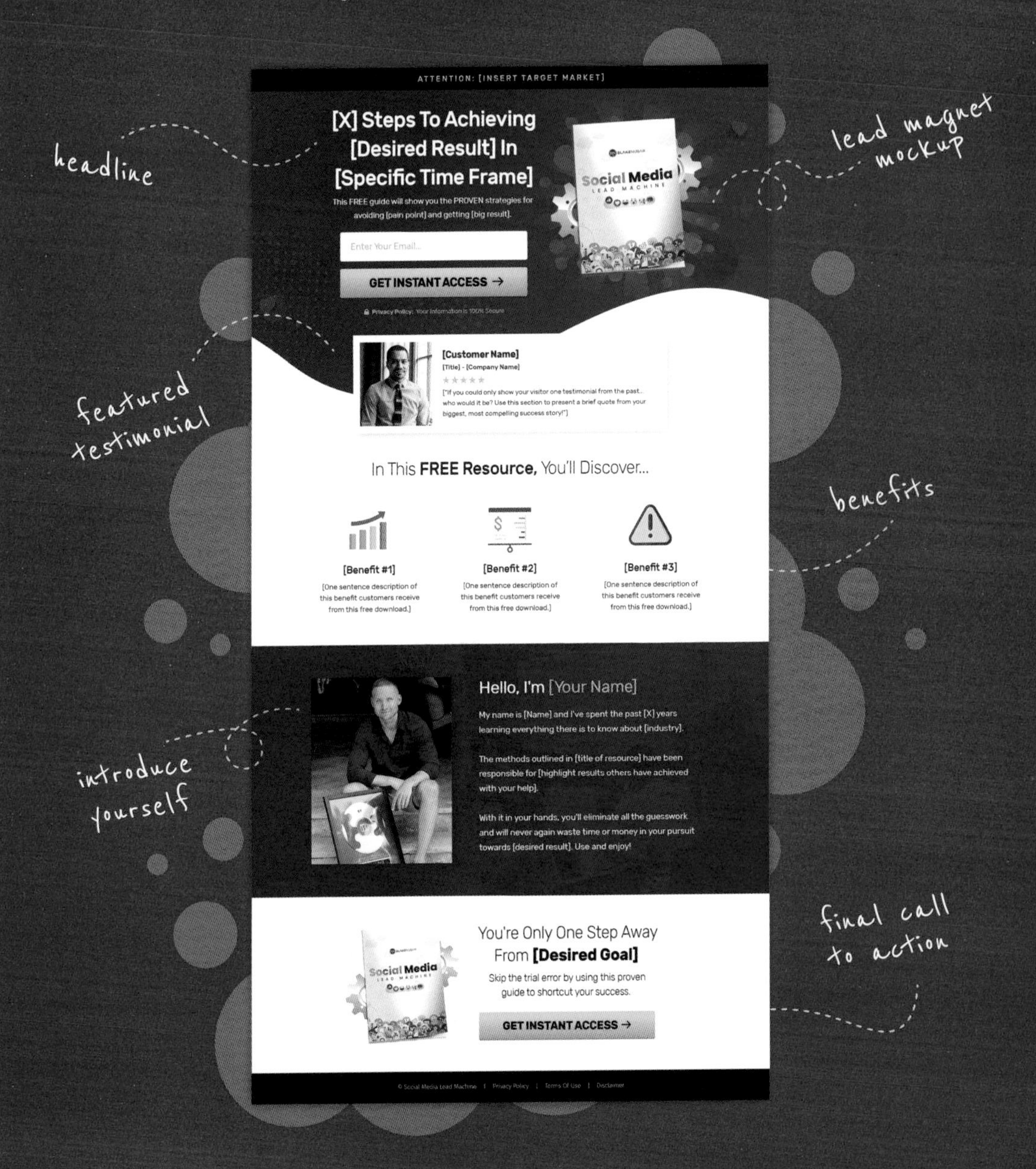


**Feel free to model this design in the landing page builder of your choice!**

# Thank you page

Once the visitor has entered their email to claim your free lead magnet, we'll direct them to the Thank You page.

**Here, we have two goals:**

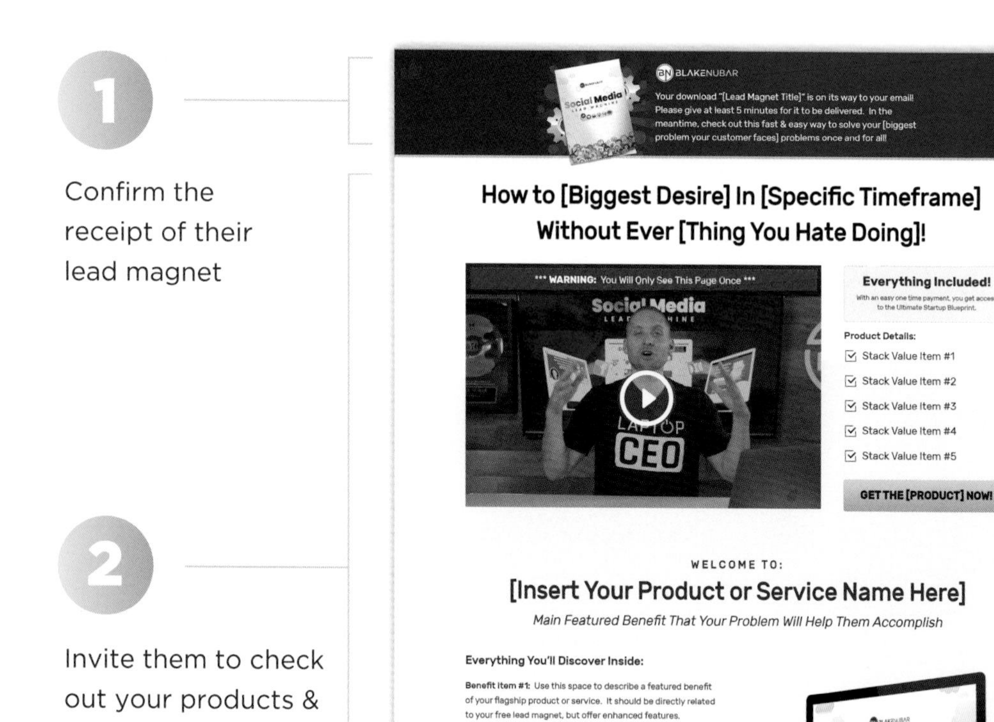


1. Confirm the receipt of their lead magnet

2. Invite them to check out your products & services, or invite them to check out your affiliate offer!

**Step 2 is where we generate income! If you already have a product or service, put the link to that page in the button here. You can also put your affiliate product link to start earning commissions just by referring your visitors from this page!**

# Your "lead machine" is offically ready to launch!

Once this is set up, your Facebook™ profile will be ready to automatically capture the "hidden visitors" from social media and convert them into paying customers!

# Your ideas

Use this page to jot down
any ideas or inspiration!

# Notes

# The 8 Step Formula

Choose a path for your online biz

Create your lead magnet

Write a persuasive call to action

Optimize your Facebook™ profile

Launch an effective landing page

Add in follow-up emails

Engage on social media

Get unlimited leads & sales!

Finish!

STEP 6

# Add in follow-up emails

# The magical power of an automated email sequence

After you generate a new lead from your profile, you'll want a set of automated emails in place to follow up and establish a connection with them!

**Trust me, without this in place...you're missing out!**

Emails sequences are a great way to drive revenue in a business. Everything is set up on timers and sent out on auto -pilot! I don't lift a finger, and these emails make me money every single day.

**DISCLAIMER:** Blake is an experienced internet marketer and his results are not typical. His experiences are not a guarantee you will make money. You may make more, less, or the same.

| STEP NAME (5) | SENT | CLICKS | ACTIVE | CTR | SALES | LIVE |
|---|---|---|---|---|---|---|
| Email #1 | 6582 | 418 | 264 | 6.35% | $9,164 | |
| Email #2 | 6240 | 173 | 92 | 2.77% | $5,422 | |
| Email #3 | 5880 | 225 | 63 | 3.83% | $2,095 | |
| Email #4 | 5305 | 259 | 125 | 4.88% | $3,576 | |
| Remove From SMLM Masterclass Abandoned Cart | 5697 | ... | 31 | ... | $0 | |



| STEP NAME (11) | SENT | CLICKS | ACTIVE | CTR | SALES | LIVE |
|---|---|---|---|---|---|---|
| Email #1 | 7110 | 498 | 251 | 7.00% | $7,936 | |
| Email #2 | 7006 | 495 | 51 | 7.07% | $6,186 | |
| Email #3 | 6146 | 323 | 191 | 5.26% | $3,040 | |
| Email #4 | 5933 | 162 | 11 | 2.73% | $1,422 | |
| Email #5 | 5803 | 206 | 7 | 3.55% | $1,199 | |
| Email #6 | 5626 | 197 | 15 | 3.50% | $2,270 | |
| SMS - Last Chance | 5403 | ... | 14 | ... | $0 | |
| Email #7 | 5412 | 300 | 0 | 5.54% | $3,307 | |

"But Blake, what kind of emails should I use for my profile funnel?"

I'M GLAD YOU ASKED

# 5-Step "Soap Opera" Email Sequence

First of all, full credit to André Chaperone for inventing the Soap Opera sequence...and to Russell Brunson for bringing it mainstream! I love this sequence because it works like magic in any niche! The goal of this sequence is to "warm up" your new leads through a powerful story that creates trust in you and your brand/products.

**Here's a quick diagram of how this sequence works:**

| DAY 1 | DAY 2 | DAY 3 | DAY 4 | DAY 5 |
|---|---|---|---|---|
| Sets the stage | High drama | Epiphany | Hidden benefits | Urgency C.T.A |
| | Backstory | The one thing | | |
| | Wall | | | |

Let's take a closer look at the 5 steps of this sequence.

# The irresistible lure of a soap opera story

If you've ever watched a soap opera, you know the feeling. With each minute that passes. the end of the episode nears and the anticipation builds.

## Then, in the last 5 minutes, BAM!

They hit you with the cliffhanger. We all know it's coming, but you still can't resist the urge to tune in next week to root for your favorite character.

This 5-Step Soap Opera Email Sequence works the same way. Only this time, **YOU are the main character of the story.** By the end of this email sequence, your new leads are waiting with bated breath to see what you have to offer them.

EMAIL 1

# Set the stage

## The Introduction

You have a matter of seconds to capture your reader's attention before they move on to the next thing...so make them count! Use the first email to introduce yourself and help the reader connect with you by sharing your personal experiences using the art of storytelling.

**Start with a little bit of intrigue to get them hooked...**

### Example: Meet John, a personal trainer

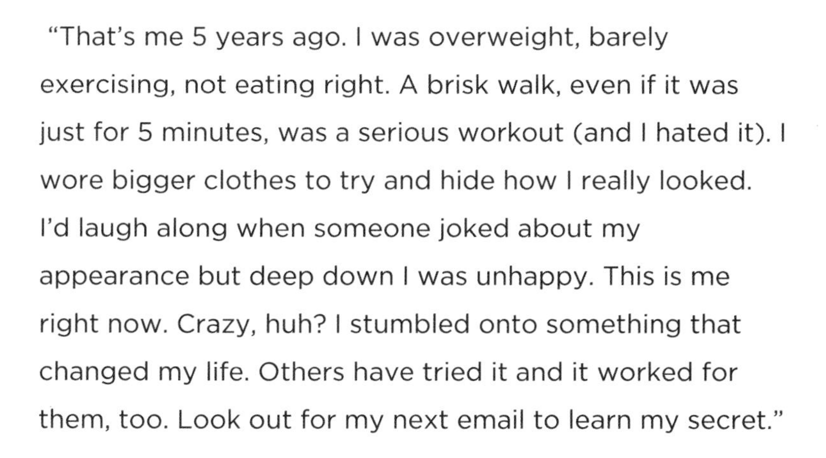

"That's me 5 years ago. I was overweight, barely exercising, not eating right. A brisk walk, even if it was just for 5 minutes, was a serious workout (and I hated it). I wore bigger clothes to try and hide how I really looked. I'd laugh along when someone joked about my appearance but deep down I was unhappy. This is me right now. Crazy, huh? I stumbled onto something that changed my life. Others have tried it and it worked for them, too. Look out for my next email to learn my secret."

EMAIL 2

# High drama

## Congratulations, you've sparked interest. The reader wants to know what you did to transform your body.

The aim of the second email is to tell your backstory to let the reader know that you understand where they're at on their journey. The best way to do this is through a backstory. Start with the highest drama point of the story and then rewind a little to explain how you ended up there.

Then, end that story with a cliffhanger by hinting at a solution to kick off the sales process.

In the final paragraph or footnote, offer more details about your secret by mentioning your product.

### Let's take an example from a real estate agent:

"I know you've been waiting to hear what my secret is. It's so simple yet provides long-lasting results. All it took was 3 months and a positive mindset. Tomorrow I'll share with you the exact steps that took me from feeling like a zero to looking like a hero."

EMAIL 3

# The epiphany

## The reader is hooked; they've connected with you, they like you, and want to learn more!

You've made it to the halfway point of your sequence. The reader finds your story intriguing and they're rooting for you. They want to know how you overcame your dilemma.

This is where you introduce the epiphany; the turning point where you found a solution (the big secret). Share a highly valuable piece of information and tie it to your product.

**By sharing details about your secret, the reader starts to see the value of your product because they've connected emotionally with you.**

EMAIL 4

# Hidden benefits

Use this email to help the reader understand how your product works for them. Try to think about your customer avatar's pains, struggles, and goals to help you define all the ways your products can benefit the reader. **Make them realize they need it!**

Don't just stop at the obvious benefits; the ones the reader figured out as soon as they read your epiphany. Detail the advantages that the reader didn't really even think of—the benefits of the benefits.

Be sure to add a call-to-action and a link to your sales page that explains fully what it is you do, how much you do it for, and how they can buy.

EMAIL 5

# Urgency/Call to action

By now, readers have learned about your product and have connected with you personally. Those who are interested have already clicked, and it's possible you've already made some sales.

This email is an urgent call to action and hits your readers with a strong, direct sales pitch. The aim is to create a sense of scarcity around your product which persuades the reader to act immediately. Make the email more enticing by including special offers with a sense of urgency, something like: "Buy within the next 24 hours and get X% off!"

Of course, you can follow up with other emails that include testimonials, a video link etc., but these five are the essentials. This sequence works because you're pulling the reader in, email by email. The strategy outlined in this book will hook in your new leads, and this email sequence will convert them from **leads into paying customers on auto-pilot!**

# Don't underestimate the power of this sequence!

This seemingly simple 5-step email sequence is one of the most persuasive tools available in email marketing! Remember - before a customer buys your product or service...they're buying YOU.

Positioning yourself as the attractive character is of paramount importance when it comes to building long-term income streams online.

## Want me to walk you through one of my soap opera sequences I use for my business?

Setting the Stage DAY 1

To

Subject **What does it take to win in [industry]?**

Hey #FIRST#,

I want to officially welcome you into my world.

The other day I got to thinking about stand-up comics and the effort they put into their performances. They make it seem so effortless, but what the audience doesn't get to see is how they painstakingly test and refine their jokes behind the scenes for a long time - sometimes for twelve straight months beforehand.

Similarly, I invested a lot of time figuring out how to succeed in **[Industry]**.

**[Back story of how you got started in your industry. Highlight the struggles and failures you faced]**

People only notice you when you come out of the other end of the tunnel. Then they say, "Oh, of course YOU succeeded - you're so awesome at this!"

But here's the good news for you: I've already done the hard work of creating an ironclad system to help you succeed in **[Industry]**.

Yes, it took me a lot of time and quite a bit of money to come up with **[company name]** but YOU can join it today... in an INSTANT.

I can say this confidently because I've yet to meet a single person who followed my simple action steps, yet didn't get results.

Keep in mind that I've worked with people of all ages, from different countries, and diverse backgrounds...

But what they have in common is that they all wanted to succeed in **[Industry]**.

If that's your attitude, then I can help you.

Do you want to find out how I can help take YOUR business to the next level? Then look out for my next email.

Thanks,
**[Your Name]**

**P.S.** The subject line in tomorrow's email is "My confidence was shattered after this - but I picked myself up." Don't miss it!

Send



**MY SOAP OPERA SEQUENCE**

I'll walk you through my personal SOAP email sequence to give you inspiration for your own!

# Download this amazing soap opera email sequence template!

## Ready to start writing your own soap opera sequence?

No need to start from scratch! Scan the code below to download my favorite template to get you off on the right track. I break down what to write in each email and how to structure the content to make your story irresistible.

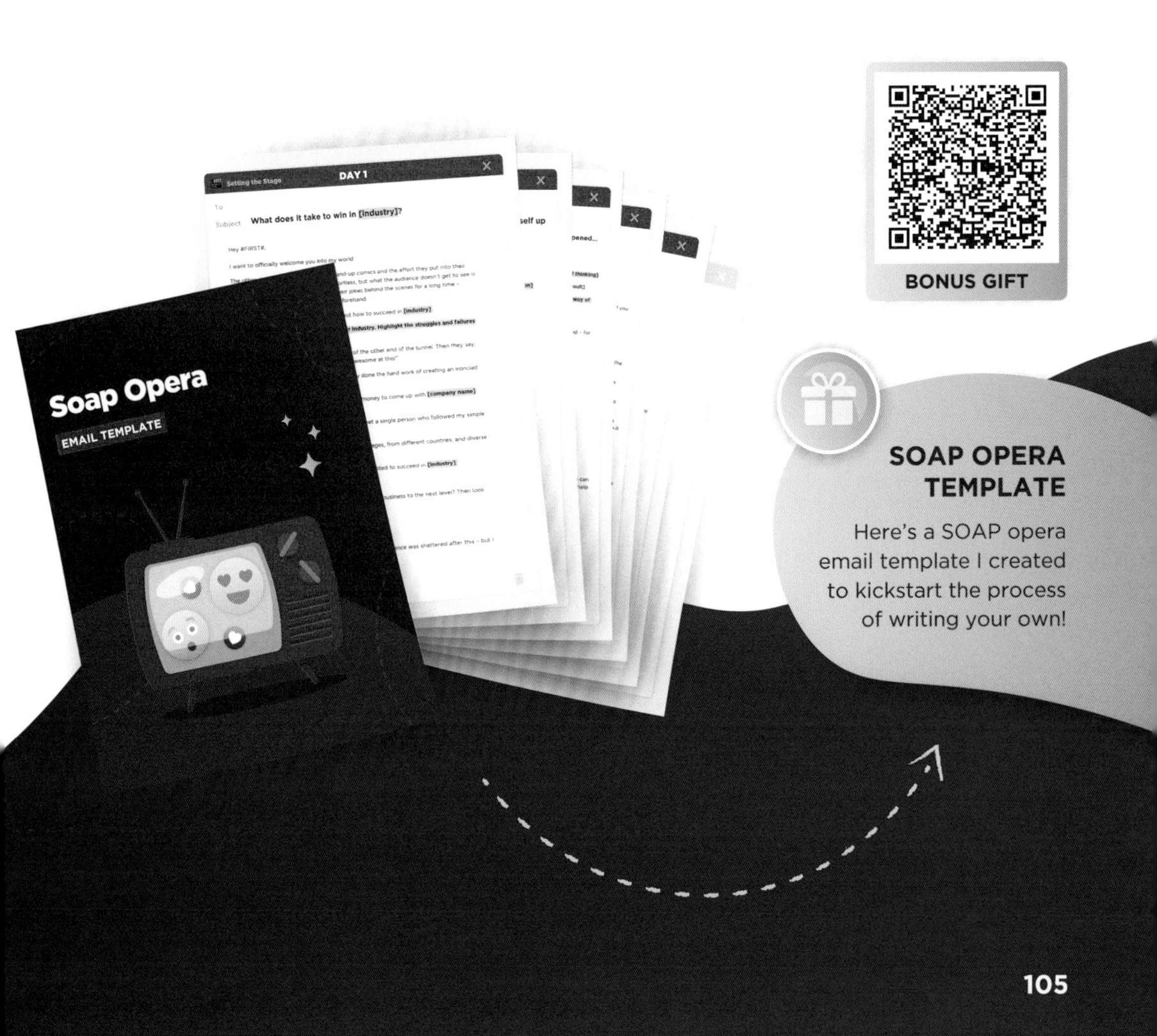

BONUS GIFT
Soap Opera
EMAIL TEMPLATE
DAY 1
Setting the Stage
What does it take to win in [industry]?
SOAP OPERA TEMPLATE
Here's a SOAP opera email template I created to kickstart the process of writing your own!

# Your ideas

Use this page to jot down
any ideas or inspiration!

# Notes

# The 8 Step Formula

Choose a path for your online biz

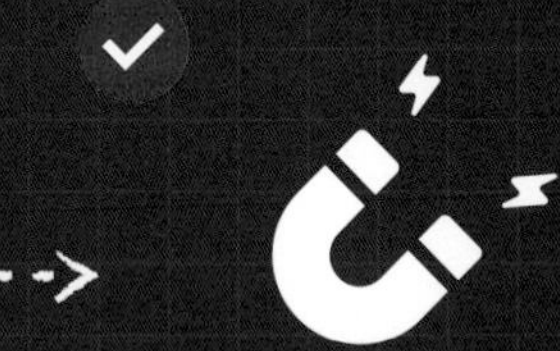

Create your lead magnet

Write a persuasive call to action

Optimize your Facebook™ profile

Launch an effective landing page

Add in follow up emails

Engage on social media

Get unlimited leads & sales

Finish!

STEP 7

# Engage on social media

# Engage on social media.

Now that your Social Profit Machine is set up...you can drive on-demand traffic to it directly from your smartphone!

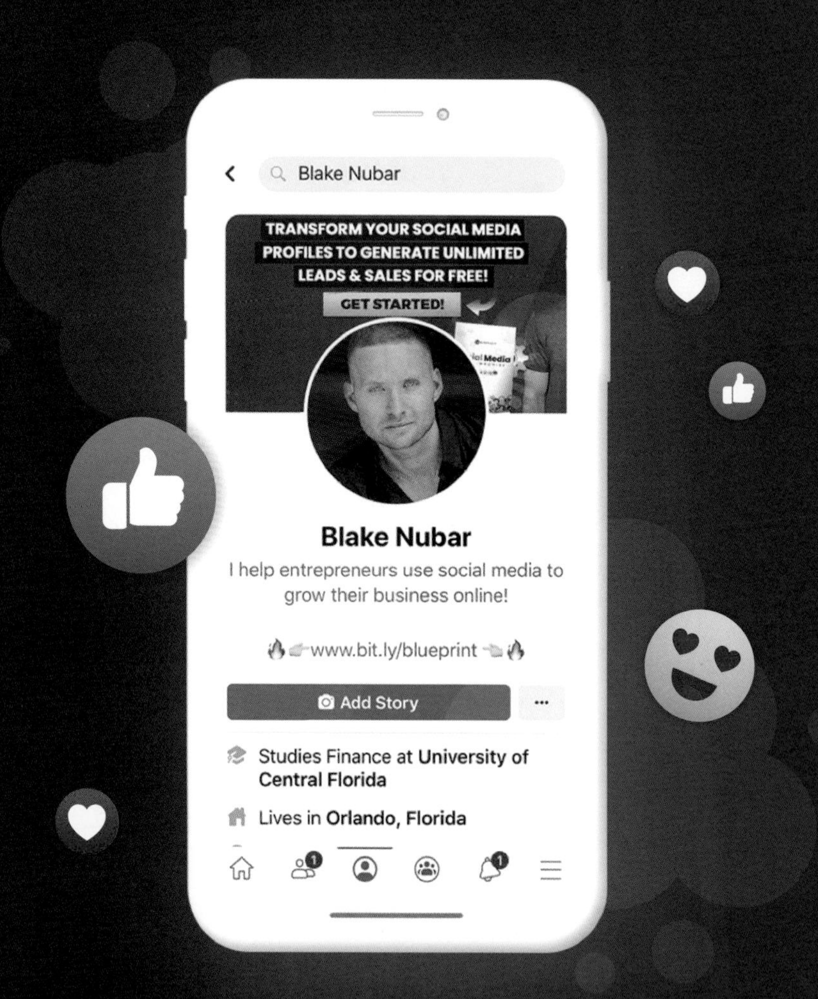


**It doesn't get any better than that!**

# Next time you have a spare moment...

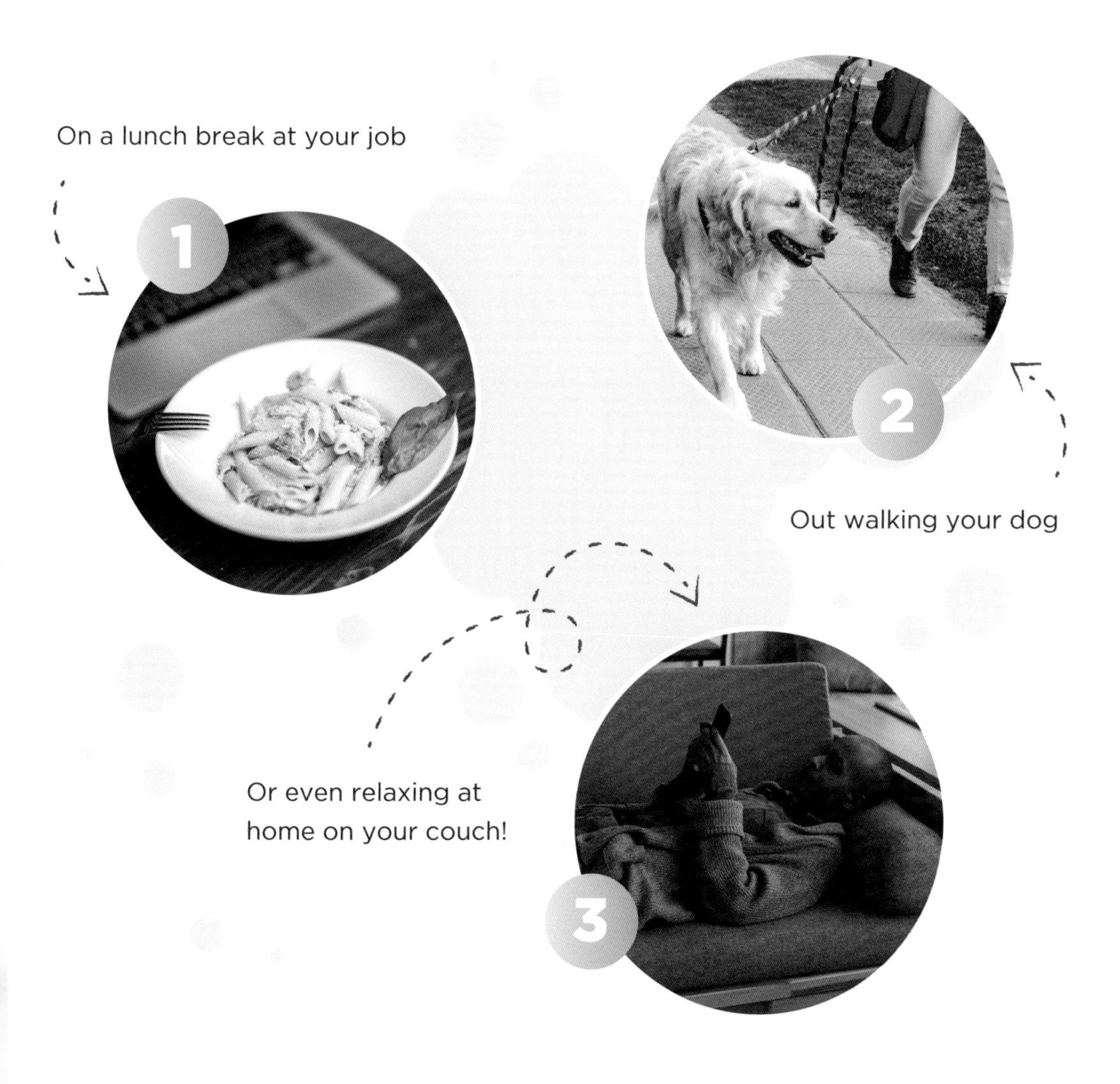

On a lunch break at your job
1
2
Out walking your dog
Or even relaxing at home on your couch!
3


**Pull your smartphone out of your pocket, open the Facebook™ app, and go interact to drive traffic! Every like, comment, share, and view now has the potential to turn into free traffic for your online business!**

# The first thing you need to do is find your watering hole.

**Facebook™ is an unimaginably gigantic place.**

Most of it is a desolate wasteland in terms of growing your business. Your key to success is finding the "watering holes" where your customers hang out every day.

## Mark Zuckerberg did us huge a favor.

Starting in 2019, Facebook™ started aggressively promoting "Groups" where like-minded people can interact in small communities.

For us business owners, this has made finding our dream customers easier then ever!

There are Groups for every niche, topic, and interest imaginable...and your future customers are hanging out inside of them every single day.

# Group "hacking"

Here's how to find Facebook™ Groups where your potential customers are hanging out in 3 simple steps.

1. Search keywords related to your business. Try to think about what topics or interests your target customer would have.

3. A list of Groups related to your business will show here. Write all potential "watering holes" down into a list!

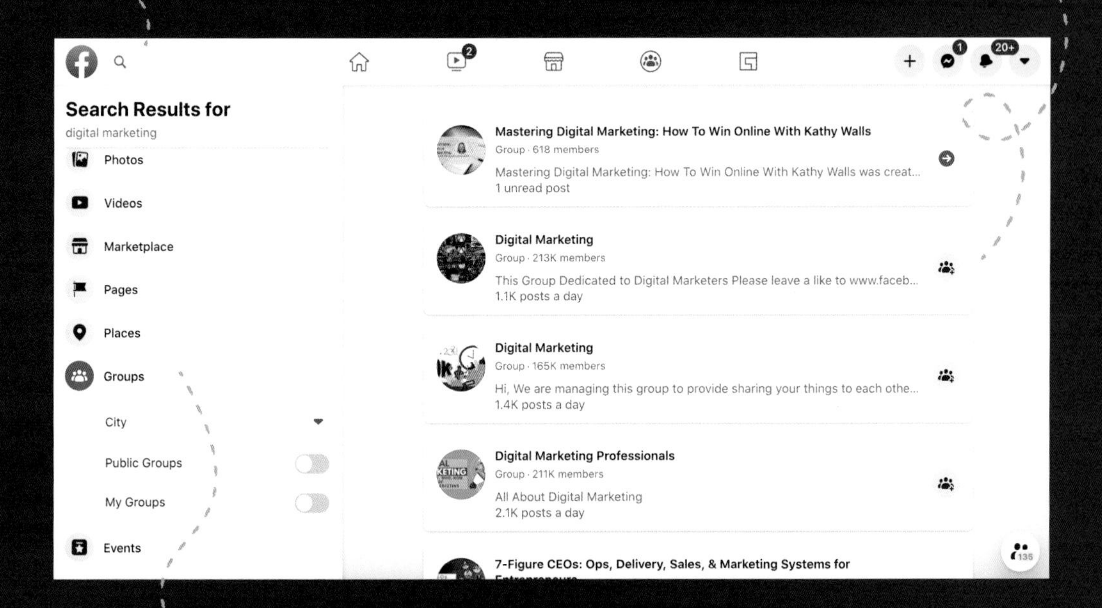


2. Select the "Groups" tab to see all the groups related to your niche! You can even sort them by city if you have a local target market.

**VALUE VIDEO**

**GROUP "HACKING"**

Here's a quick tutorial on how to easily find Facebook™ Groups filled with your dream customers!

# Flashlight < Laser Beam

Now, I know you might be thinking, "Wow...this is awesome! I'm going to join every group out there related to my business!"

I don't recommend doing that. You'll see much better & faster results if you narrow your focus and invest all your energy into a select few.

So, whittle down your list and **choose the top 3 groups you want to participate in.**

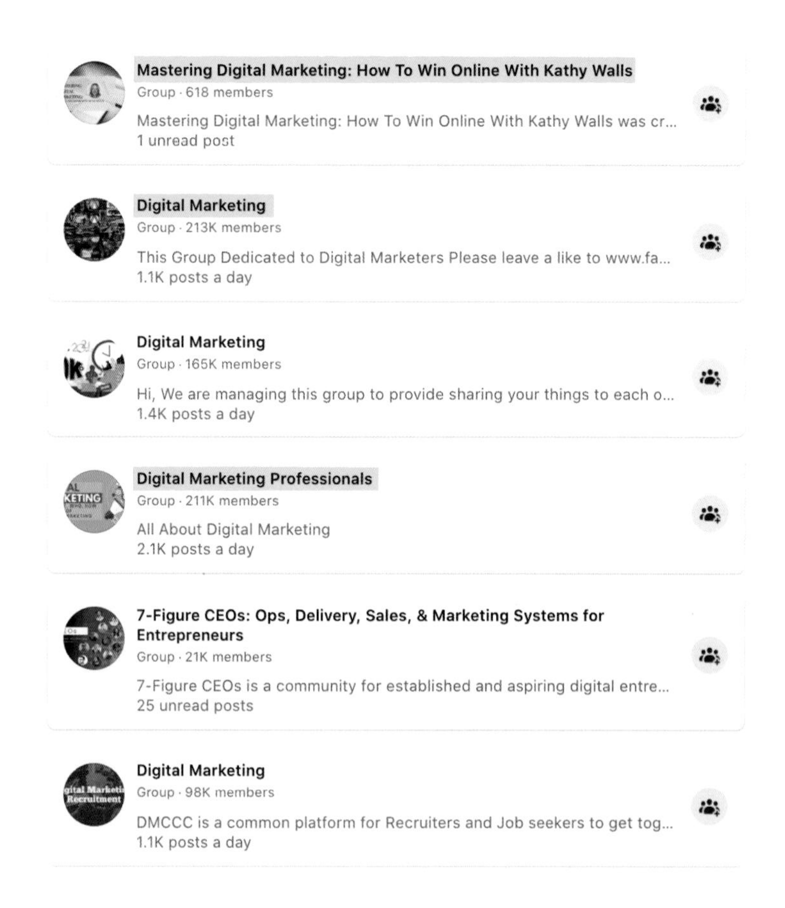

Join groups and interact!

# 3 easy ways to drive unlimited traffic!

## 1 Interact on social media.

Inside these groups...every like, heart, and comment drives highly targeted traffic straight to your profile and into your funnel.

## 2 Post content related to your niche.

By posting valuable content into groups, you quickly establish yourself as the go to "authority" on all topics related to your business.

## 3 Network with Messenger.

In these groups, you're bound to virtually "meet" new potential customers. Message them and start building the relationship, then ascend them directly to your products & services!

# 1 Interact on social media.

## Watch for golden opportunities.

Your gut instinct may tell you to watch for posts that go "viral" and wait to engage with those.

But posts that don't have any engagement are often your best opportunities to shine. A like, heart, or comment on a post with ZERO attention will naturally pique the curiosity of the person who posted it FAR more than one that already has a frenzy of engagement.

**Be the superhero that swoops in to save the day and you'll quickly build a tribe loyal followers.**

## Provide value.

I know it sounds counterintuitive, but I can personally vouch that this is true.

Your fastest path to growing influence, building an audience, and ultimately monetizing it is to **help people for free and ask nothing in return.**

You'll be amazed by how much this strategy pays off in spades over time.

# Become a farmer, not a nomad.

Nomads are typically searching for the "quick win" and will sacrifice long-term gain in exchange for immediate gratification.

On the other hand, farmers are patient individuals that plant seeds now...knowing they will come to fruition in the future.

**If your goal is a consistent and robust source of new customers from social media, it's time you start adopting the "farmer" approach to your business.**

# 2 Post content related to your niche.

Posting valuable content on your profile and inside the groups you participate in will quickly help position you as a thought leader in your niche.

**Make sure your content is thoughtful, relevant, and helpful to your potential customers!**

**Here are some Facebook™ post ideas that will help get your creative juices flowing on what content to post for your business!**

**7 VIRAL POSTING TEMPLATES**

Use these 7 done-for-you Facebook™ post templates to give you inspiration on what to post!

# Not sure what to post to attract new customers?

BONUS GIFT

## 7 viral posting templates

Use these 7 templates to help get your creative juices flowing and break the ice in Facebook™ groups you plan on interacting in!

## Post types

- Ask campaign
- Value bombs
- Know the squad
- Fill in the blanks
- Term of the day
- Share a win
- A day in the life

# 3 Network with Messenger.

4:43

Allison
Active now

As you begin to join & interact in Facebook™ Groups related to your business, you'll begin to attract new people into your orbit.

When you make a new connection, reach out via messenger to introduce yourself!

That personal touch creates an open line of communication and establishes instant rapport... there's a human on the other end of that message, and you're at their fingertips the next time they need help!

Aa

# There are 1.3 billion people on Messenger

Facebook™ Messenger is like texting, but more intimate - which also makes it HIGHLY effective as a networking tool to build relationships at scale.

Plus it's ENORMOUS! And it remains largely untapped for entrepreneurs like you.

# Hire a virtual assistant.

## Don't want to spend the time doing all this yourself?

Here's the good news - this is a task you can outsource to a Virtual Assistant so that you can put this entire system on 100% autopilot.

Take the template provided on this page, customize it for your business, and post a job on Upwork or Fiverr to find someone to fill this role.

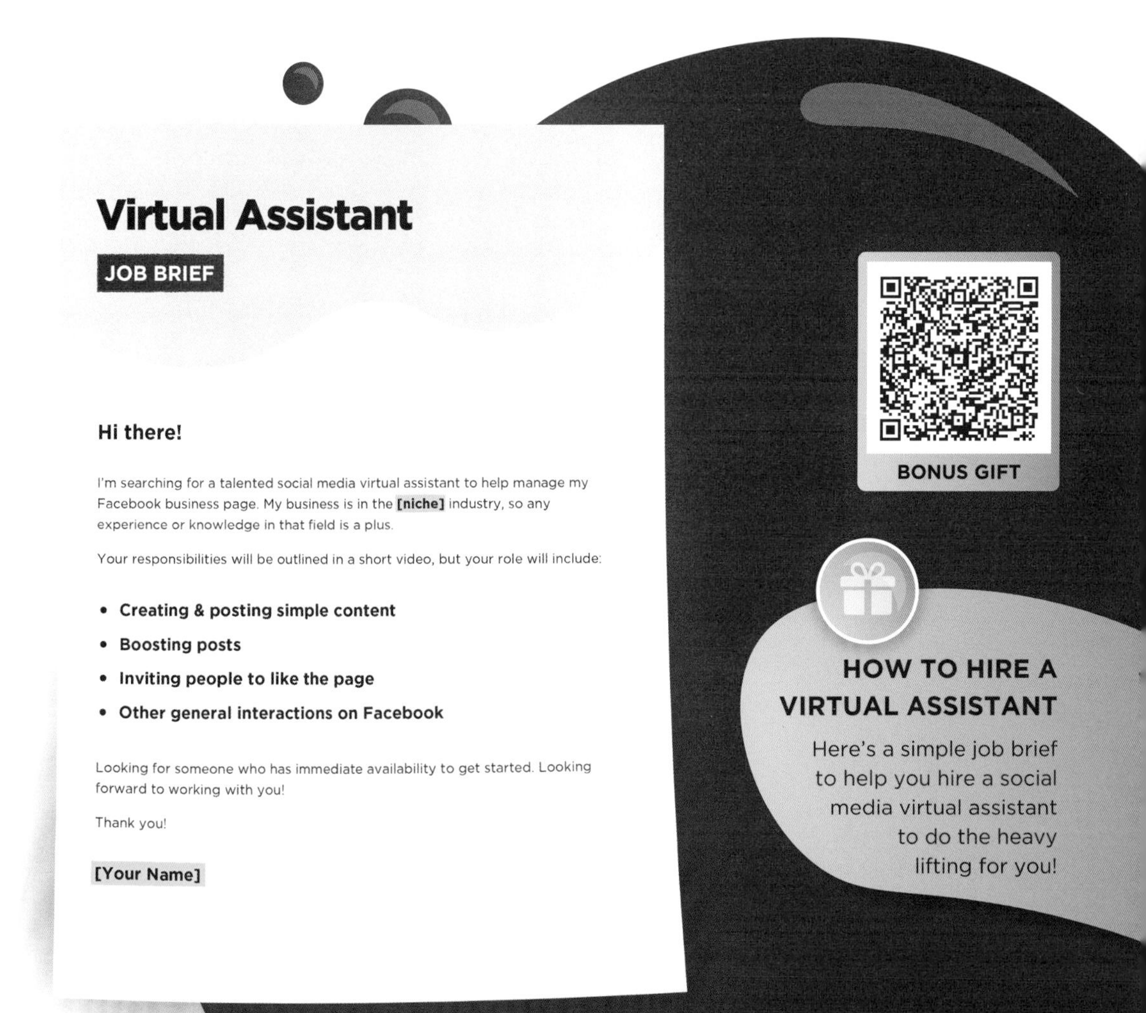
Virtual Assistant

JOB BRIEF

**Hi there!**

I'm searching for a talented social media virtual assistant to help manage my Facebook business page. My business is in the **[niche]** industry, so any experience or knowledge in that field is a plus.

Your responsibilities will be outlined in a short video, but your role will include:

- **Creating & posting simple content**
- **Boosting posts**
- **Inviting people to like the page**
- **Other general interactions on Facebook**

Looking for someone who has immediate availability to get started. Looking forward to working with you!

Thank you!

**[Your Name]**

BONUS GIFT
HOW TO HIRE A VIRTUAL ASSISTANT
Here's a simple job brief to help you hire a social media virtual assistant to do the heavy lifting for you!

Your ideas
Use this page to jot down
any ideas or inspiration!

# Notes

# The 8 Step Formula

Choose a path for your online biz
Create your lead magnet
Write a persuasive call to action
Optimize your Facebook™ profile
Launch an effective landing page
Add in follow up emails
Engage on social media
8
Get unlimited leads & sales!
Finish!

STEP 8

# Get unlimited leads & sales!

# Congratulations!

**You've now created a fully automated system that siphons off FREE leads & sales from your Facebook™ profile!**

1. Interact on social media (you can do it from your smartphone!)
2. Transform your profile into a "landing page" that offers visitors an irresistible, free offer
3. Link your profile to a simple landing page where visitors enter their email to claim your irresistible freebie.
4. Deliver on your promise by sending the free offer and inviting your visitors to your paid products & services

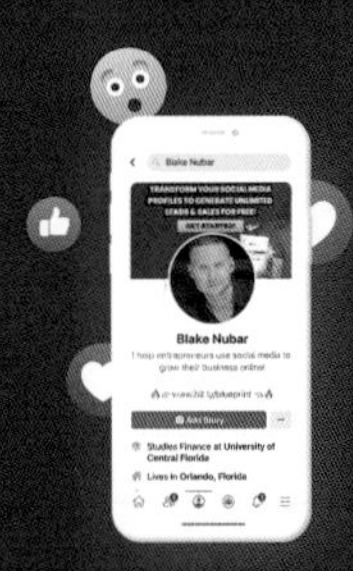

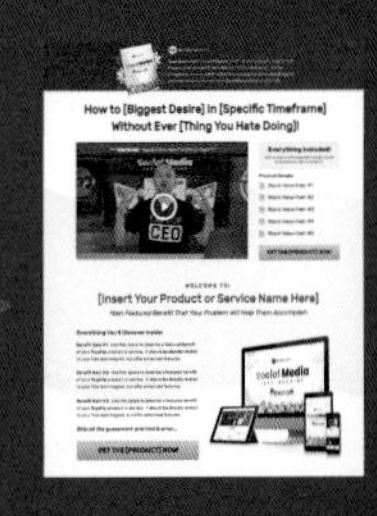

5. Ascend your visitors to your paid products & services and generate income on auto-pilot, just by interacting on social media!

AT THIS POINT YOU MIGHT BE THINKING...

# What's next?

Dear Overachiever,

First of all, I want to congratulate you on being a motivated action taker.

I talk to entrepreneurs every day who have the desire to start a business that will change their life, but few have the guts to put their plan into action.

Just by ordering this book, you've shown that you're serious about getting real results. For that reason, I want to do everything I can to help you make your goals a reality.

That's why I want to extend a special invitation to work directly with me, so that you can finally get an online business up & running that gets the results you're looking for, launch a business that inspires and creates value for others, and have a plan that works for the long-run so you can gain that "laptop lifestyle" freedom we all desire so intensely.

**If that appeals to you, then you're invited to a 100% free training that shows you exactly how to do just that!**

# What you will learn on this 100% free training:

www.SecretBonusTraining.com

### Secret 1

A revolutionary "franchisable" internet business that lets you clone a sales funnel, put your spin on it, and launch it for yourself!

### Secret 2

Tap into this "fish in a barrel" source of customers that's wide open for the taking on the largest social media platform in the world!

### Secret 3

One simple button that allows you to run this entire business from the convenience of your pocket!

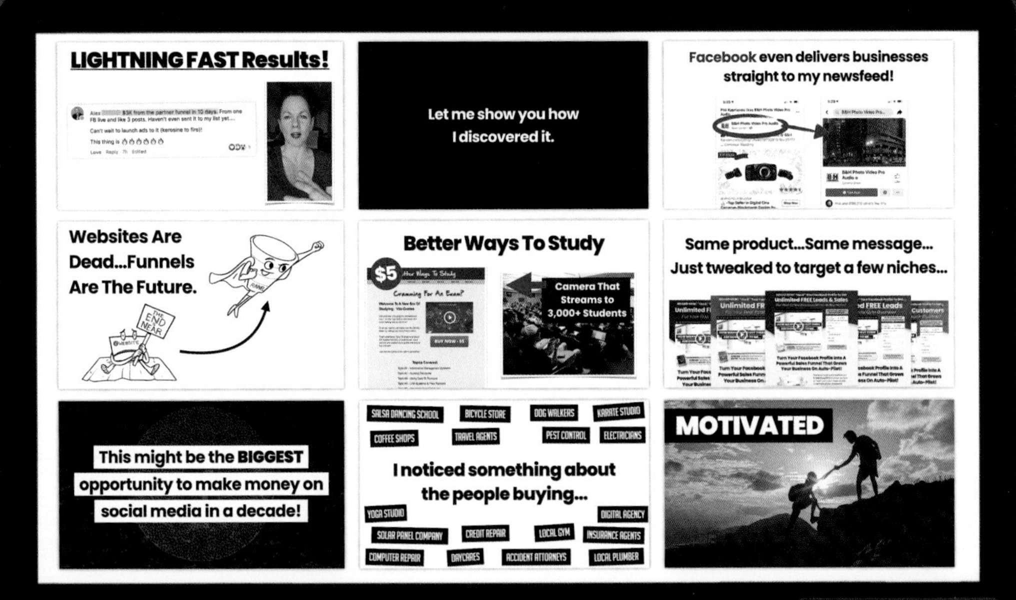

VALUE VIDEO

**FREE BONUS TRAINING!**

Get instant access to my epic bonus training that's included with your purchase!

# Now here's my promise to you.

Trust me - I've attended countless workshops that pack the first 30 minutes with fluff [eye roll].

I can assure you that this is nothing like that. I respect your time and get straight to the point in showing you the "good stuff" about a brand new opportunity to work with me to launch your online business in record time.

Once you combine the steps from this book with the actionable strategies from my free training, you'll be an unstoppable force online (even if right now you're starting from scratch!)

## So what are you waiting for?
## You have nothing to lose!

**Visit www.SecretBonusTraining.com and get started immediately. I can't wait to work further with you, open your eyes to the wealth of opportunities the internet has to offer and crush it online!**

# About the author

Blake Nubar is an entrepreneur in Orlando, Florida. He entered the world of funnels and internet marketing a few short years ago and has since helped thousands of people achieve financial freedom using sales funnels.

In 2017 he co-founded a digital marketing agency with his business partner, Ace Glenn, that specializes in marketing strategy and funnels. With a keen eye for what "works" and an obsessive passion for design, Blake has been able to achieve extraordinary success for himself and the clients he works with in a short period of time.

**"In all my time as an internet entrepreneur and working with thousands of people just like you, I've never seen a better way to find success online than with the Social Profit Machine".**

# Interactive QR code index

In case you missed a few while reading the book, you can easily scan all the interactive content on the next few pages!

Page 1

*Value Video*

### Special Video From Blake!

Let me show you how this interactive book works and how to get the most out of it!

Page 8

*Value Video*

### From Broke To Millions

Check out my backstory to see how I went from struggling & broke to earning millions online!

Page 11

*Value Video*

### Hidden Social Media Traffic

You won't believe how many people do this to YOU every single day!

Page 12

*Value Video*

### 3D Profile Animation

Watch how your profile can transform with this epic animation. If a picture is worth 1,000 words, this is worth a million!

Page 17

*Value Video*

### See Jaw-Dropping Results

Hear from of entrepreneurs just like you who have grown their businesses online.

Page 27

*Value Video*

### How Affiliate Marketing Works

Blake will break it down in a simple way so it's easy to understand!

Page 28

*Useful Website*

### ClickBank Affiliate Products

Sign up for ClickBank and see all the affiliate products you can earn commissions from!

Page 29

*Bonus Gift*

### Customer Avatar Worksheet

Download this customer avatar worksheet to help nail down your niche!

Page 38

*Useful Website*

### PLR Store Lead Magnets

Browse through the SUPER affordable done-for-you lead magnets available in the PLR store!

Page 39

*Bonus Gift*

**Lead Magnet PSD Templates**

I created these epic lead magnet photoshop templates to make it easy for you to get a stunning result quickly!

Page 40

*Useful Website*

**Browse On GraphicRiver**

For endless inspiration, visit www.graphicriver.net and search keywords related to your business!

Page 41

*Useful Website*

**Outsourcing Made Easy**

Visit Fiverr to hire an affordable designer to create your lead magnet mockup.

Page 41

*Bonus Gift*

**Job Brief Example**

Download this simple job brief to let your designer know exactly what you want for your mockup!

Page 51

*Bonus Gift*

**My Favorite Headline Template**

Download an editable version of my favorite headline template and fill in the blanks to create your own!

Page 53

*Useful Website*

**Browse Emoji Options**

Check out the HUGE number of different emojis that you have to choose from!

Page 54

*Value Video*

**How Link Trackers Work**

Learn about useful software that helps you track "link click activity" on your profile!

Page 55

*Bonus Gift*

**Headline Brainstorming Worksheet**

Use this worksheet to brainstorm different headline ideas for your lead magnet!

Page 66

*Value Video*

**How To Optimize Your Profile**

Let me show you exactly how this profile system works!

Page 71
*Value Video*

### Animate Your Profile Pic

Bring your profile to life with an eye-catching video created with this unique mobile app!

Page 86
*Useful Website*

### Try ClickFunnels Today!

Test drive the world's leading funnel building platform! It's perfect for beginners.

Page 96
*Value Video*

### Shocking Email Results

You'll be SHOCKED by the results I generate from automated emails!

Page 104
*Value Video*

### My SOAP Opera Sequence

I'll walk you through my personal SOAP email sequence to give you inspiration for your own!

Page 105
*Bonus Gift*

### SOAP Opera Template

Here's a SOAP opera email template I created to kickstart the process of writing your own!

Page 115
*Value Video*

### Group "Hacking"

Here's a quick tutorial on how to easily find Facebook™ Groups filled with your dream customers!

Page 122
*Bonus Gift*

### 7 Viral Posting Templates

Use these 7 done-for-you Facebook™ post templates to give you inspiration on what to post!

Page 125
*Bonus Gift*

### How To Hire A Virtual Assistant

Here's a simple job brief to help you hire a social media virtual assistant to do the heavy lifting for you!

Page 134
*Value Video*

### Free Bonus Training!

Get instant access to my epic bonus training that's included with your purchase!